Pertinent wisdom
from the folks in charge

Hillary

"It's time for a new beginning, for an end to government of the few, by the few, and for the few, and to replace it with shared responsibility for shared prosperity."

"(We) can't just let business as usual go on, and that means something has to be taken away from some people."

"We have to build a political consensus, and that requires people to give up a little bit of their own turf in order to create this common ground."

"I certainly think the free-market has failed."

"I think it's time to send a clear message to what has become the most profitable sector in (the) entire economy - that they are being watched."

"We are going to take things from you for the common good."

Carter Glass

"A liberal is a man who is willing to spend somebody else's money."

Saul Alinsky (Chapter one on Training Community Organizers)

"What follows is for those who want to change the world from what it is to what they believe it should be. The Prince was written by Machiavelli for the Haves on how to hold power. *Rules for Radicals* is written for the Have-Nots on how to take it away". (Rules for Radicals, a Pragmatic Primer for Realistic Radicals)

Arpege perfume advertising slogan:

"Promise her anything, but give her Arpege."

Rush Limbaugh

"Liberal Democrats are inexorably opposed to tax cuts, because tax cuts give people more power, and take away from the role of government"

Nancy Pelosi

"We need to work toward the goal of equalizing income, in our country and at the same time limiting the amount the rich can invest.

"We need to raise the standard of living of our poor, unemployed and minorities. For example, we have an estimated 12 million illegal immigrants in our country who need our help along with millions of unemployed minorities. Stock market windfall profits taxes could go a long way to guarantee these people the standard of living they would like to have as 'Americans.' "

"If we don't have an economic recovery package, five hundred million Americans lose their jobs." (this out of a population of 301 million!)

Barack Obama

"I think that when you spread the wealth around, it's good for everybody"

Barack Obama 1/25/07 "We will have universal health care (read socialized medicine) in this country by the end of the next president's first term."

"Under my plan of a cap and trade system, electricity rates would necessarily skyrocket... whatever the industry was, uh, they would have to retrofit their operations. That will cost money. They will pass that money on to consumers."

"If anybody wants to build a coal power plant, they can, but it will bankrupt them."(about 50% of our electricity comes from coal)

Tom Daschle (1998):

"Tax cheaters cheat us all, and the IRS should enforce our laws to the letter." (Mr. Daschle withdrew as President Obama's Secretary of HHS nominee in 2009 because he was a $140,000 tax cheat.)

Charles Schumer

"Democrats don't relate to middle-class people."

Progressive Caucus Position Paper

"We propose the introduction of a package of legislative initiatives that will close America's economic divide and address both income and wealth disparities."

P. J. O'Rourke

"If you think health care is expensive now wait until you see what it costs when it's free".

J. Paul Getty

"The meek shall inherit the earth, but not its mineral rights."

Barbara Boxer

"We are not going to be big brother or sister, as the case may be." on government

John Maynard Keynes

"The avoidance of taxes is the only intellectual pursuit that carries any reward."

Ludwig Von Mises

"Nothing is as ill founded as the assertion of equality of all members of the human race."

Thomas Jefferson

"The natural progress of things is for government to gain ground and for liberty to yield."

Robert Higgs

"By adopting programs to redistribute substantial amounts of income, a nation guarantees that its government will become more powerful and invasive in other ways."

Variously attributed to Winston Churchill, George Bernard Shaw, Benjamin Disraeli and Otto Von Bismark

. "If you are not a liberal when you are twenty-five, you have no heart. If you are not a conservative by the time you are forty, you have no brain."

William S. Lind

"If we compare the basic tenets of political correctness with classical Marxism the parallels are very obvious." , from An Accuracy in Academia Address.

Joan Rivers

"I told my mother-in-law that my house was her house and she said, 'Get the hell off my property'."

Mark Twain

"There is no distinctly native American criminal class save Congress."

Chuck Holmes

"The leading cause of mental illness in the United States today is being elected to Congress."

Rush Limbaugh

"Regulators ordered a Kansas City bank to install a Braille keypad on its drive-through automatic teller machine, presumably to aid any blind drivers."

J. H. (PaBoy) Holmes (my father)

"You can't tell how rich a man is by how much money he has. You have to look at how much he owes."

Sol Luckman

"Begging is much more difficult than it looks. It's a high art form that takes years of dedicated practice to master."

P. J. O'Rourke

"You can't get rid of poverty by giving people money."

What Kind of People Spend our Money for Us?

The exact composition in Congress varies from session to session, but it stays somewhat around the following.

- 36 have been accused of spousal abuse
- 7 have been arrested for fraud
- 19 have been accused of writing bad checks
- 117 have directly or indirectly bankrupted at least two businesses each
- 3 have done time for assault
- 71 cannot get a credit card due to bad credit
- 14 have been arrested on drug-related charges
- 8 have been arrested for shoplifting
- 21 currently are defendants in lawsuits, and
- 84 have been arrested for drunk driving in the last year

Source: Series of articles at chblue.com
Since there is turnover, this is vague on specific parties, and numbers, but it remains about the same from Congress to Congress. see further discussion at http://www.truthorfiction.com/rumors/c/congressionalcriminals.htm

Politically Correct Economics

A Semantic Primer for Realistic Radicals

Selling the Same Old Socialism
Under the Banners of
"Hope" & "Change"

Charles W. Holmes, PhD

Heuristic Books
Chesterfield, Missouri USA

Graphics Credits:
The cover design and other graphics are by Robert J.
Banis, Ph.D., based on various government and internet
sources which we believe are public domain. Please let
us know if you find errors
March, 2009

ISBN 9781596300224 paperback
Electronic PDF version ISBN 9781596300569

Library of Congress Cataloging-in-Publication Data
Holmes, Charles W. -1932-
 Politically correct economics : a semantic primer for
realistic radicals selling the same old socialism under the
banners of "hope" & "change"/ Charles W. Holmes,.
    p. cm.
  ISBN 978-1-59630-022-4 (regular print : alk. paper) -- ISBN
978-1-59630-056-9 (eBook(pdf))
 1 Economics. 2 Political Correctness 3 United States —
Economic Policy.   I. Title

 HB171.5 .H695 2009
 330 22

                                                2009012217

Heuristic Books
PO Box 7151
Chesterfield, MO 63006-7151
(636) 394-4950
heuristicbooks.com

Dedication

For Merelyn, my wife of fifty-three years.

For my daughter Donna Hellums and husband Don, my granddaughter Courtney Suber and husband Jamey, and my new great grandson Trent Suber, who will be paying for the Pelosi/Obama//Reid spending spree the rest of their lives.

And Dr. Bud Banis, CEO of Science and Humanities Press, who did a magnificent job in putting this book together.

An Afterthought

This book was not intended to be about Barack Obama. I began jotting down the principles that became the Manifesto of Politically Correct Economics some ten years ago, some time before I knew there was a budding politician named Barack Hussein Obama. I was writing a parody of what the economy would look like when the politically correct took over. Mr. Obama is a perfect fit. There is not one of the articles of the manifesto that he does not support. After observing Mr. Obama's first few weeks in office, it would seem that I have unintentionally written the first book on Obamanomics

Table of Contents

FOREWORD

This is a book of tongue-in-cheek satire and humor. Because the target audience is composed of all concerned Americans rather than the academic elite, I have decided to not confuse the reader with footnotes and references to seldom-read academic journals. Those who want to confirm most of my information and data may easily do so by referring to the World Almanac, the Internet or the Statistical Abstract of the United States. Other information I merely remember.

Political correctness was born during the late seventies and early eighties as a reaction to the success and offensive nature of current society. As the Greek philosopher and historian Polibius said, "...every democracy which has enjoyed prosperity for a period" must expect some sort of rebellion against the existing order. Hippies found it offensive that the current culture in the United States found hippies offensive. They thought the Vietnam War, which they blamed on conservative Republicans, offensive. They rebelled against the existing order by burning their bras and draft cards.

Today's rebellion is in the form of Political correctness. The totalitarian purpose of political correctness is to prevent behavior or speech, and even thinking, offensive to groups currently in favor of the politically correct. No words or behaviors should offend women, blacks, homosexuals, the obese, the handicapped, the lazy, Muslims and anyone who may be considered "different." It is permissible to use speech or behaviors to offend, punish and silence white males, conservative Republicans, Christians, Jews, educated minorities and successful businesspersons. Political correctness is an enemy of academic freedom as students shout down conservative lecturers or any other authoritative figure with whom they do not agree, and defend those who say, with emotion their only evidence, that the government of the United States destroyed the World Trade Centers by implosion and blew holes in New Orleans levees to kill people during hurricane Katrina. Anita Vogel of Fox News reported that textbook reviews in states across the country have eliminated references to "everything from founding fathers to hotdogs," distorting and changing history in the sake of political correctness. Attempts have been made to get "Dr. Laura" off television because of her views on homosexuality. Students at Brown University destroyed thousands of copies of a newspaper because they considered an ad against reparations for slavery in the newspaper racist. Other universities that ran the ad were forced to apologize. One university refused to apologize, saying to do so would violate free speech. Efforts to ban books because of their "offensive" content are ongoing. Leading liberals and intellectual giants of Hollywood, some educated, some who barely finished high school and one notable who did not, eagerly support the claims and efforts, however irrational, of the politically correct. Even more frightening, the politically correct have gained support from leaders of Congress, both in the House of Representatives and the Senate.

Political correctness has been the subject of ridicule, but it is far from ridiculous. Politically correct police, working under the principle of mob rule, at first enforced unwritten laws of their own making. Unwritten law later became written law or administrative policy. Political correctness as we know it today has been around for only a few years: de facto political correctness has existed for a century or more. Fifteen million people starved to death in Russia during Stalin's collectivization of agriculture in the late 1920's. Ten million more were exiled or imprisoned in work camps, with many never to be seen again. All in the name of political correctness, Marxist style. During the holocaust, in what Adolf Hitler called "the cleaning (die Reinigfung)," more than five million Jews were victims of the Nazi's own version of political correctness. Millions of other "undesirables" were killed. Political correctness carried to the extreme can be a scary thing indeed. Political correctness is liberalism. What's really scary is that liberals are now in charge.

This book is an attempt to ridicule that which is not ridiculous. I am going to make fun of the politically correct approach to economics. When the politically correct take over, this is the way the economy will work. This is the way economic problems will be defined, interpreted and solved.

Politically Correct Economics can well serve as a concise primer for basic economics because economics principles discussed here are valid. The economic problems are real. However, problem definition and their resolutions are strictly politically correct and have no relationship to reality. Indeed, my greatest fear is that someone, somewhere, sometimes, will take seriously any definition of problems or any solutions recommended here.

Chuck Holmes, Ph.D. 2009

GLOSSARY OF POLITICALLY CORRECT ECONOMICS

The following are generally accepted politically correct terms that apply to economics. Their origin is difficult to determine but their use is common among both advocates of political correctness and those who oppose the movement. For a complete list of politically correct terms, see *The Official Politically Correct Dictionary and Handbook* by Henry Beard and Christopher Cerf, published by Villard Books of New York. Some of these are contained therein*. Most are remembered from reading various articles, the names and authors of which I no longer remember. Some I made up myself because I thought they were appropriate for the subject.

ABILITY-TO-PAY PRINCIPLE OF TAXATION The only equitable way of distributing the tax burden. All excess income of the economically privileged should be taxed away for subsequent redistribution to the economically marginalized and differently motivated. The economically marginalized and differently motivated are excused from paying taxes because they have no ability to pay.

BENEFITS RECEIVED PRINCIPLE OF TAXATION Provides that those who receive the

7

benefits of public goods should pay taxes. This includes tolls, gasoline tax and other use taxes.

BUREAUCRACY A large governmental organization with many employees called bureaucrats. The primary purpose of such an organization in a benevolent government is to establish rules by which wealth is redistributed from the economically advantaged to the economically disadvantaged and the motivationally deficient.

CAPITAL An economic resource. An aid to production of goods made in a factory by humyn laborers. Capital includes all machinery and tools used in production.

CAPITALIST An oppressive business owner who advocates a market economy.

COMMUNISM A politically correct, classless society where all are equal and each contributes according to ability and consumes according to need.

DIFFERENTLY-ABLED* Mentally retarded, handicapped

DIFFERENTLY-FOCUSED* Avoiding reality, emotionally handicapped.

DIFFERENTLY MOTIVATED Lazy.

ECONOMIC CYCLES Periods of recession, during which capitalist oppressors acquire property at low prices, and periods of inflation, during which they sell the property at high prices. Usually caused by political meddling with the money supply.

ECONOMIC EMPOWERMENT Wealth

8

ECONOMIC EXPLOITATION   Payment of wages which are less than the value of labor. A weapon used by economically advantaged capitalists.

ECONOMIC RESOURCES   Land, labor, capital and entrepreneurship. Also known as factors of production.

ECONOMICALLY ADVANTAGED Rich

ECONOMICALLY MARGINALIZED* Poor

ECONOMICALLY OPPRESSED   Poor. Any humyn who works for an economic oppressor and receives wages.

ENTREPRENEUR   A humyn who combines other resources and bears the risk of production. An oppressive capitalist.

FISCAL POLICY   Changes in government spending and taxation to bring about equality among all humyns. A secondary purpose is to stabilize the economy, eliminating periods of recession and inflation.

FRIVOLOUS LUXURIES   Consumer items purchased by the economically advantaged to impress their neighbors; includes boats, expensive cars, motor homes, video cassette recorders, large television sets, cameras and beef steak.

GRAY-MATTER   CHALLENGED Unintelligent, dense, dull, obtuse.

HANDSOMELY DEFICIENT Ugly

HER'M'IT Contraction of the nonsexist, non-animality specific her or him or it.

9

HE'S'HI'TS   Contraction of nonsexist, nonanimality specific hers or his or its.

HI'R   Contraction of the nonsexist his or hers, or his or her

HOMELY-DEFICIENT   Pretty or handsome

H'ORSH'   Contraction of nonsexist he or she

H'ORSH'IT*   Contraction for the nonsexist, nonanimality specific he or she or it. (My favorite, from *The Official Politically Correct Dictionary and Handbook*)

HOUSEHOLDS   Individual or family units that provide resources to the economy and use payments received for these resources to purchase consumption goods and services. Households consist of both oppressors and the oppressed.

HUFEM*   A vaginal humyn

HUMYN*   Nonsexist spelling of human

LABOR   Humyns who earn meager wages while working for capitalist oppressors.

LAND   An economic resource that occurs in fixed quantities and is a gift of nature. Land includes all dirt along with all the gold, iron, coal and other minerals therein. Land as a natural resource even includes water.

LEGALIZED INCARCERATION   The state in which a married wofem exists.

MALE SEX OPPRESSOR   Husband

MARKET   In a capitalist economy, the place where buyers and sellers meet. The market benefits only the economically advantaged, for the economically marginalized have nothing to sell and cannot afford to buy anything.

MIDDLEMEN Humyns who enrich themselves at the expense of others. They buy goods at less than just prices and sell them at higher than just prices.

MONETARY POLICY The manipulation of the money supply by the Federal Reserve System so that capitalist bankers may borrow money at low interest rates during recessions and lend the money to the economically oppressed at high interest rates during periods of inflation.

MOTIVATIONALLY CHALLENGED Lazy

MOTIVATIONALLY DEFICIENT* No incentive to get ahead.

NONVAGINAL HUMYN A male humyn

OPPORTUNITY COST That which is given up to obtain something else. If a humyn decides to have pizza instead of hamburger for lunch, the cost of the pizza is the hamburger. Economists see opportunity cost as the true cost of anything.

PERSON Literally means "through the son" and is considered a politically incorrect, sexist term. Should always be replaced by the word "humyn."

PHYSICALLY CHALLENGED* Handicapped

SIGNIFICANT OTHER* Husband, wife, boyfriend, girlfriend. Generally must be a live-in.

TRUTH DEFICIENT A lie

UNPAID DOMESTIC SEX PROVIDER Wife

USURY   The charging of excessive interest rates by oppressive bankers when lending money to the economically marginalized.

UTILITY   In economics, utility simply means "satisfaction."

VAGINAL HUMYN   A female humyn

WAITRON   Nonsexist term for waitress or waiter

WIMYN*   Nonsexist spelling of women

WOFEM*   A womyn

WOMYN*   Nonsexist spelling of woman

THE MANIFESTO OF POLITICALLY CORRECT ECONOMICS

1. All humyns, other than white nonvaginal humyns, are created equal.

2. It is the responsibility of the government to ensure that all vaginal humyns remain equal to one another and superior to white nonvaginal humyns.

3. Nonhumyn members of animality, especially snail darters, spotted owls, marsh mice and California brush rats have more economic rights than white nonvaginal humyns.

4. Capitalism is inferior to all other economic systems.

5. The capitalist market is an invention of economic oppressors and is therefore basically wicked. The market will always benefit the economically privileged who control it.

6. The economic laws of supply and demand benefit only the economically advantaged and should be repealed by Congress.

7. Money is the leading cause of inequality and is the bane of the economically challenged.

8. Economic freedom cannot exist as long as any vaginal humyn anywhere is oppressed.

9. The primary economic responsibility of the Federal, state and local governments of the United States is the redistribution of income and wealth from the privileged classes to the economically marginalized and differently motivated.

10. No individual humyn is responsible for her or his own economic well-being. It is society as a whole that bears ultimate responsibility.

11. Any humyn who works for another humyn in order to receive wages is oppressed.

12. A large benevolent government will solve all of society's economic problems.

13. Economic freedom is essential for all humyns. A strong central government must be empowered to impose, by force if necessary, freedom on the entire population.

14. A beneficent government is in a better position to know what is best for private citizens than are citizens themselves.

15. All economically oppressed humyns have the basic right of home ownership.

16. As long as any humyn is homeless, no other humyn should be allowed to own more than one home.

17. All humyns are entitled to free medical and dental care.

18. All humyns are entitled to a free education through a Ph.D. or the professional school of their choice.

19. Society must constantly instill feelings of guilt in successful, independent economic oppressors.

20. The primary purpose of the economy must be to improve the economic condition of the economically exploited and differently motivated.

21. Each humyn, regardless of ability or motivation, is entitled to an equal share of all goods and services produced by the economy of the United States.

22. The current monetary system of the United States is unconstitutional and should be replaced with a system of vouchers which may be exchanged for specific goods and services.

23. The power to tax is the most powerful weapon available to a politically correct government.

24. The primary purpose of any system of taxation must be to bring about equality among all citizens.

25. Government should never implement tax cuts because the humyns might see the benefits of lower taxes and demand even more tax cuts.

26. Government should never cut spending because such cuts will lead to diminished government power.

27. Only when the United States Health Care Delivery Service is administered with the reliability and efficiency of the United States Postal Service will health care be affordable and available to all.

28. Government must use the power of eminent domain to seize private property and make it available for use by all humyns.

CH 1:ECONOMICS AND WHAT ECONOMISTS DO

Two of the great mysteries of modern humynkind are, What is economics? And, What do economists do?

Economics, along with political science, psychology and sociology are all considered "social sciences," but are really not sciences at all. Even as disciplines, they are rather inexact. Of all these nonscience disciplines, economics is probably the most inexact. The discipline of economics is so inexact that Harry Truman once said that he wanted a one-armed economist. He wanted a one-armed economist because the one who worked for him would always say, after offering one answer to a question, "But on the other hand... ."

Most economists of today are politically incorrect and it is rather difficult to specify exactly what it is that they do. One characteristic common to all economists is that they are always ready to answer any question that may be asked. As Harry Truman found out, they will, just to cover all bases, nearly always provide more than one answer. The provision of several answers to a given question constitutes a politically acceptable approach to problem solving and is not seen as a problem by most politicians. They can choose the answer that best fits their current mood, or perhaps choose the one that provides the best chances for reelection.

Economists are not only willing to give several different answers, they will confidently provide answers to questions about which they know nothing, and will quite willingly answer questions which have nothing to do with economics. It doesn't matter that they don't know the correct answers. Economists answer questions for the same reason mountain climbers climb mountains. They answer questions merely because they are asked!

Politically incorrect economists are also prolific predictors of the future. They like to predict future events about as much as they like to answer questions. History has shown, however, that economists are as proficient at predicting the future as they are at providing one correct answer to a given question. Someone once observed that god created economists to make weather forecasters look good. Notice that we use a non-capitalized "g" in the spelling of god. This indicates a nonanimal specific, gender-neutral, general-purpose politically correct god that (rather than "who" because we are not sure that god is of humyn form) would be acceptable to all religions and denominations. Such nonspecificity is absolutely essential if any scholarly work such as this is to be accepted by the elite faculty and administrators currently charged with educating the young in our modern American universities. A noncapitalized spelling of god is also considered nonoffensive. The politically correct are extremely sensitive to others and do not wish to offend anyone except those who disagree with the PC movement.

It has been observed that economists correctly predicted seven of the last three recessions.

Economists usually, but not always, predict things that have something to do with economics. It is therefore necessary, in order to be more specific about what economists do, to first establish what the inexact science called economics is. This is no small task because even economists cannot agree on a single definition.

Economics is an academic rather than vocational subject. A humyn can attend vocational-technical school for a year or two and be awarded a certificate in auto mechanics. That humyn can immediately go out into the community and mechanic. One may get a certificate in plumbing and then start to plumb. One may attend a college or vocational school, get some sort of degree or certificate in bookkeeping and keep books.

It is not true in economics. One must attend college for at least four years and take courses in macroeconomics and microeconomics and finance and international finance and money and banking, along with the required humynities, English and history courses which are concerned only with the accomplishments of dead white European males.

Students of economics also have to take a course in calculus (which is a type of uppity mathematics) for economists. For the most part, real mathematics majors don't consider calculus for economists to be real mathematics. In schools of business, it is called "business calculus." Other schools, those in which mathematics and science are taught, real mathematicians refer to the course more appropriately as "baby calculus."

The calculus course has one purpose--to enable the future economist to write long calculus equations to put in their economics journal articles. Economists include such equations in their articles on the assumption that if any subject includes enough mathematics, it can be considered a science, and to be a scientist means to have prestige. The equations contain many meaningless combinations of Greek symbols and lower-case letters of the English alphabet. Nearly never are any actual numbers placed into the equations.

The mostly politically incorrect journals in which economists publish their articles are sponsored by associations of mostly politically incorrect economists. It is a convenient arrangement because a minimum number of published articles is required if economists want to keep their jobs as college professors. But the arrangement is not unique to economists. Associations of physicians, sociologists, psychologists and lawyers have been formed to provide the same service for their respective professions. Such associations are necessary because articles written by economists and other professionals could not be sold for a profit through the market system that politically incorrect economists advocate.

Yet, after one takes all required university courses, joins the appropriate national and regional economics associations and publishes scholarly articles, there is no way h'orsh'it can go immediately out into the world and economic, while plumbers can go out and plumb.

A brief explanation, for the benefit of the politically incorrect, is appropriate at this time. The word *h'orsh'it* is not intended to be offensive nor is it intended to be obscene. It is the politically correct, nongender specific, animality neutral term for he or she or it. The term is used here not only to include females in what was once a male-dominated profession, but also to not limit those who can be economists to humyn beings. Economists have at times been referred to as "pigs" or "being chicken." At other times, economists are often referred to as horses' asses.

Back to the task at hand. In trying to establish exactly what the dismal science called economics is, we find that a review of only a few standard economics textbooks reveals several definitions.

One popular definition is that economics is *the study of production, exchange and consumption of goods and services.* This definition is not often used, probably because it makes too much sense and does a pretty good job of describing what economics is.

Another popular way of defining the dismal science is that *economics is the science of constrained maximization of choice.* This definition is more popular among economists for two reasons. First, it requires extensive elaboration (by an economist) before anyone understands it. The second reason it is popular is that it provides credibility to the economics profession by describing economics as a science. It also justifies the use of that list of calculus formulas economics students developed while attending graduate school.

The meaning of the definition is based on the assumption that the wants of an avaricious society are virtually insatiable. Consumers want food, shelter, clothing and frivolous luxuries such as cars, boats, televisions, cameras and motor homes. Businesses want investment goods such as factories, computer systems, office buildings, furniture, coffee pots and production lines so that they can make their obscene profits. Government wants office buildings, post offices, furniture, coffee pots and foolish military goods such as guns, tanks, airplanes and aircraft carriers.

Choices must be made because the economy cannot possibly provide everything that is wanted. When we choose to have one thing over another, that which we do not choose is called opportunity cost. Economists like to think of cost as what must be given up to buy something else, rather than the actual amount of dollars spent to make the purchase.

According to this definition, the bases of the choices of society are invariably attempts at maximization of something.

When we private citizens make our choices, we want to maximize our personal satisfaction, which economists prefer to call utility. Suppose, for example, we have ten dollars to buy lunch for five days. We can choose a hamburger or hotdog at a cost of two dollars each. We choose the one that we think will give us the most satisfaction. If we choose a hot dog, the true cost of that hot dog is one hamburger rather than two dollars because we lose the opportunity to purchase a hamburger. The problem with utility is that the oppressed

American wage earner makes so little money that maximization of satisfaction is of little concern. Their choice is generally one of necessity. For two dollars, enough bologna can be purchased to provide lunch all week.

Business, when making its choices, attempts to maximize profit. That is why American businesses are building factories and shipping jobs overseas to countries where goods can be produced by impoverished workers. American workers would like a living wage, a wage that would allow the worker to choose between a hamburger and a hotdog for lunch. But Mexican workers are willing to work all day for the same wage Americans want each hour, or even for a few tortillas. Chinese workers may demand only a cup or two of rice. This cuts production costs considerably and increases profit for oppressive American business owners. It also increases inequality and poverty, adding to the already large class of oppressed workers as their jobs rather than the products they could make are exported.

What about governments? State, local and Federal officials claim that they are attempting to maximize social welfare when they make choices about how to spend taxpayers' money. If this were true, our politicians and government would be behaving in an acceptable politically correct manner. Why aren't they? Governments are composed of politicians and bureaucrats. Politicians are interested only in trying to maximize their chances of reelection. They will invariably do those things that have immediate and visible benefits for large blocks of American voters, but have hidden or deferred costs to taxpayers, all of which require massive amounts of government spending. The purpose of which is to buy the votes of their constituents and ensure their reelection.

Bureaucrats, since they are not elected but are career government employees, try to maximize power. Why else would the chairman of General Motors Corporation (a fantasized example only) give up eight (or possibly nine) figures in income, place all accumulated wealth in a blind trust, and take a job as Secretary of Transportation? A job which was in 2005 limited by law to an annual salary of only $180,100, a mere fraction of the bureaucrat's income prior to government service? The lust for power, of course. At GM, power can be exercised only over GM and its employees. As Secretary of Transportation, power can be exercised over transportation systems of the entire nation as well as Ford, DaimlerChrysler, Toyota and other foreign companies which import or manufacture motor vehicles into the United States.

What is the constraint under which consumers, business and government officials make choices? The scarcity of economic resources, say economists. Resources are scarce, they say, only because our wants are virtually insatiable. This reveals the true political incorrectness of current economic thought. Only the economically advantaged are constrained in their wants by scarcity of resources. The economically marginalized, including the mentally and physically challenged and the differently motivated, are exploited by economically advantaged oppressors and are constrained by the lack of money. It is paradoxical that economists don't consider money to be an economic resource.

24

They consider only land, labor and capital as resources.

Land is defined as any unimproved natural resource that occurs in fixed quantities. Land therefore consists of the thing we know as land, but by definition is also iron ore, crude oil, gold and even water.

Capital was once defined as any man-made aid to production. After enlightened and politically correct students in colleges and universities throughout the United States pointed out that the term "man-made" is sexist and insensitive to the role of vaginal-Americans, economists began to define capital as manufactured aids to production. The word "manufactured" is also sexist because it literally means, "made by man in a factory." The sensitive intellect of today prefers a more politically correct definition that does not exclude the contribution of vaginal-Americans and nonhumyn animals. We prefer to define capital as *aids to production made in a factory by h'orsh'it.*

Labor is the mental and physical efforts of humyns and nonhumyn animals. We are all laborers; doctor, lawyer, native-American chief, rich humyn, economically marginalized humyn, beggar-humyn, thief and Budweiser Clydesdales as they pull the Budweiser beer wagon through the Christmas snow. The economically marginalized should constantly remind oppressors that economic exploiters are also laborers in addition to their status as privileged professionals.

Many economists identify a fourth resource, the entrepreneur. The entrepreneur combines the other resources, innovates (finds newer and cheaper ways to produce) makes major decisions and bears the risk of production. Without this unit of animality, nothing would be done because h'orsh'it is the driving force behind all production and is therefore the ultimate oppressor.

It is interesting that money, contrary to what most humyns of normal intellect would think, is not capital. Money is not considered an economic resource because it doesn't produce anything. Money is money only because the government says it's money and humyns are willing to accept it in exchange for goods and services. Money, in and of itself, has no value and is worth only what one can get with it. If a humyn animal possessed all the money in the world, h'orsh' would not have any satisfaction. Money provides satisfaction only when it is spent. Besides, if one humyn had all the money in the world, the rest of the world would be on some other medium of exchange and that money would be worthless. So say economists, anyway.

Money, therefore, has no intrinsic value because it provides no direct satisfaction. Yet, when some economist wins the Nobel Prize, what does h'orsh' get? MONEY! The economist then makes lengthy public statements of how much satisfaction will result from the money. We can again see the brilliance of politically incorrect economic thought!

Regardless of what economists say, money is the leading cause of inequality and is the bane of the economically challenged.

There are other definitions of economics, but most are variations of the second and deal with the problem of getting the most we can from our limited economic resources.

To the real-world oppressed, however, economics is just trying to get along in life. The major constraint is money. The barrier is inequality. The culprits are successful oppressors who will not share their wealth with the differently advantaged and motivationally deficient.

There are essentially two basic types of economics--socialism and capitalism. There is a third--communism--which is really nothing more than an extension of socialism. Communism (when spelled with a capital C) is more political party than economic system and currently exists only in Cuba, North Korea, China, and on American University campuses, but is coming of age in Venezuela. Communism seemed to have died in the place of its birth, Russia, and other Eastern European countries during the oppressive Reagan administration. Now, however, it may be on the comeback as Eurocentric humyns, the Asian identified and our neighbors in South America begin to experience the economic exploitation commensurate with the capitalist market system.

Communism also seems to be in trouble in the American university system, once considered a safe habitat. Because of the politically correct movement, Communism is losing out to multiculturalism and is therefore becoming less of a political issue. Even the great oppressor Reagan could not accomplish that! The politically correct see this as an improvement because, unlike communists, multiculturalists do not attempt to foster revolutions in other parts of the world. They merely attempt to make those places where they currently live as much as possible like the places they left.

The differences in the three types of economic systems can be comprehended through a simple example.

Suppose an egg farmer has fifty hens. In a Communist economic system, the government would seize the hens and then distribute eggs to all citizens, including the farmer, on the basis of need. The farmer would still have to care for the hens, feeding them and gathering eggs which h'orsh'it would turn over to the government. Under socialism, the farmer would continue to own the hens, but still would have to sell the eggs for a mere pittance to the government, which would distribute them, again on the basis of need, to all. Under capitalism, the farmer would sell one of the hens and buy a rooster, ensuring a continuing supply of eggs to be sold to the economically advantaged at an obscene profit.

It is obvious why capitalism is not an acceptable economic system. After the capitalist farmer acquires roosters, the remaining hens will become subject to male domination and be nothing more than oppressed, unpaid sex providers.

Other reasons why capitalism cannot be an acceptable economic system lie in its basic philosophy. The underlying principle of capitalism is the concept of private property, meaning that private individuals can actually own things. They can own their own land, homes, cars and even uniquely American products known as bass boats. Bass boats are frivolous luxuries found only in advanced capitalistic societies. They are of no practical use and offer no benefit to society as a whole. Capitalists may keep their private property until they get tired of it and then dispose of it in any way they see fit. Even after they die, capitalists can sustain ownership of property in their families through the right to bequeath, leaving their possessions to their heirs in a will. Society as a whole is thereby denied the opportunity to acquire the property for the benefit of all.

The right to bequeath property also leads to child and family abuse. Capitalist owners of business often require that their children actually work in the family business in order to inherit that business. Otherwise, oppressive parents may accuse their children of being undeserving and sell their businesses before they die. The now more advantaged parents will dispose of their wealth by purchasing frivolous luxuries such as recreational vehicles, boats and waterfront condominiums to enjoy during their retirement. They rationalize that if their children don't want to work for the family business, parents might as well enjoy their last years by spending their children's inheritance. Legitimate heirs are then denied their rightful inheritance, merely because they may be motivationally deficient, and will be unable to redistribute the wealth to the economically deprived who really deserve it.

Another of the underlying principles of capitalism is economic freedom. Business, it is believed, should be able to produce whatever products it wants to produce, consumers should be able to buy the products they want to buy, and workers should be able work where they choose to work. The major problem with freedom is that businesses will always choose to produce products that will provide the greatest amount of profit. These products are usually those that are desired by white, male, insensitive oppressors who are also the ones who own other businesses. Capitalists produce only for one another! Oppressive business owners hold underpaid slave surrogates in bondage by not giving them an equal share of profits, further increasing inequality and denying workers a means of lateral mobility. Workers therefore do not experience economic freedom as such because they cannot afford to work where they choose.

Capitalism is a market economy. All major economic decisions--what will be produced, the production methods to be used and who will receive the benefits of production (including the actual goods produced)-- are made by the market. This is seen as particularly mean-spirited because decisions made by capitalist oppressors are invariably based on PROFIT! Capitalists will always produce those things that can be sold for the most profit. They will use least-cost productive methods, even though this means that jobs will be moved out of the United States to lesser-developed countries where severely oppressed humyns are willing to work for pennies a day. Goods will be provided only to people who are willing and able to pay the obscene prices demanded by oppressive business owners. To produce goods more cheaply means more profit. To require people to pay for goods means profit. Capitalists have little regard for people who would like to have some of the same frivolous luxuries such as sport-utility vehicles, yachts, bass boats and motor homes that the economically advantaged have. The economically oppressed do not have the means to pay for them.

Capitalists believe that, since economic decisions are to be made by the market, the government should take a "hands-off" approach to the economy. Any attempt by the government to assist in the economy, even if the purpose is to bring about equality among all, is seen by capitalists as interference rather than assistance.

The politically correct believe that it is the responsibility of the government to make all economic decisions. Capitalists criticize this as socialism and, in their often-desperate attempts to justify a market-driven economy, relate stories of inefficiency in economies driven by government benevolence. One such story is about toasters and the decision of the Russian central planning committee to manufacture them.

During the early eighties, a leading financial journal contained an interesting story about toasters in Russia. Russia, in spite of the existence of the so-called Cold War, was still trying to westernize its social structure (history tells us that the Russians have foolishly been trying to do this since the days of the Czar). One of the many Russian teams visiting the United States at the time had as an objective the task of determining the major difference between typical American and Russian households. (There was a lot of visiting back and forth of Russians and Americans during those days.) President Carter rightly thought that if Americans knew and understood the Russians, they would learn to love them. The Russians thought that if their people, not realizing that they already lived in a politically and economically perfect world, could be more like Americans they might be less rebellious.

After visiting in several American homes, the team returned to Russia and reported to their commissar that the one major difference was a toaster! Every American kitchen had a toaster sitting on the counter. As far as members of the junket knew, no family in Russia had a toaster. If Russian families were to be more like American families, they had to have toasters.

The decision was made. The manufacture of toasters would receive high priority in the Gosplan, the five-year economic plan of the Soviet Union. Enough toasters would be manufactured so that every family in Russia could have one. Parity between American households and Russian households would finally be achieved!

There was one rather major problem in the production decision. Since goods such as toasters had until then been considered frivolous luxuries, no plans for their manufacture were available in the Soviet Union. Toasters manufactured in Russia would therefore be modeled after a sample brought back by the visiting Russian team. It was one of the pop-up types, with slots for two pieces of sliced bread, made by several small appliance manufacturers in the United States. Millions of similar toasters were built, enough so that every household in Russia could become more westernized.

That none of the Russian families bought the toasters, nor even wanted them when they were offered for free, does not indicate a failure of the Russian economic system as capitalist oppressors maintain. It is simply that Russian householders were not ready for capitalist toasters. Nor was Russian bread. The toasters were designed for American style, pre-sliced bread such as Americans buy in prepackaged loaves at capitalist supermarkets. Russian bread is generally baked in large, sometimes round, loaves and is not pre-sliced. Even when sliced, the bread is too large to fit into the small openings of the capitalist toaster.

Regardless of the perceived minor problems, it stands that enough toasters were manufactured so that each Russian household could have one. This would never happen under a profit-driven capitalist economic system. Many economically challenged families in the United States do not have a toaster to this day because they cannot afford to pay for one!

Let us return to our two original and key questions. What is economics and what do economists do?

Economics is and has been a pseudoscience concerned with making choices. Economics attempts to answer the questions: What is to be produced and in what quantities? What is to be the means of production? Who will get the benefit of the products produced in the economy?

In a market-based economy, first described by Adam Smith in 1776, industrialists will produce those things from which they can maximize profit. They will use least-cost production methods and distribute the items to those who are willing and able to pay, again so that they can maximize profit. Little consideration is given the economically marginalized.

If non-goal-oriented members of society are to be afforded the same opportunities as overachieving oppressors, the market-driven economy must be considered an institution of the past. The economy is dynamic. What worked in Adam Smith's day may not be appropriate now. Social programs implemented by Franklin D. Roosevelt and the great humynitarian, Lyndon Baines Johnson, have proved to be successful but need to be expanded. President Clinton and his wife Hillary, the senator from New York and possible President of the United States, were rebuffed in their attempt to bring free medical care to all Americans. So it is not only new social programs that are needed, but better education programs to indoctrinate the politically incorrect so that they will not oppose progressive social change.

Only since the mid-nineteen eighties have the politically correct been making themselves heard, primarily within American educational institutions. They are a force that capitalist oppressors must eventually deal with.

So what is economics? What do economists do? Economics is "what economists do," according to one astute economist. A professor of medicine I once encountered on a fishing trip, after learning that I was a professor of economics said, "Oh! That is a course in college where the questions on the end-of-course examinations always remain the same. Only the answers change." It stands to reason that the economist is the one who changes the answers.

John Maynard Keynes provided a different perspective. He wrote in 1933 that an economist must:

"possess a rare combination of gifts. He must be mathematician, historian, statesman, philosopher-in-some-degree. He must understand symbols and speak in words. He must contemplate the particular in terms of the general, and touch abstract and concrete in the same flight of thought. He must study the present in light of the past for purposes of the future. No part of man's nature or his institutions must lie entirely outside his regard. He must be purposeful and disinterested in a simultaneous mood; as aloof and incorruptible as an artist, yet sometimes as near the earth as a politician."

WOW!

Perhaps the definition of economics given by John Kenneth Galbraith is the most appropriate:

"Economics is extremely useful as a form of employment for economists."

CH 2: THE POLITICALLY CORRECT ECONOMIST

The economic philosophy of the politically correct is liberalism. Liberalism stands for individual freedom--of religion, of speech and of conscience. The politically correct may worship whomever or whatever they want, say what they want and feel guilty of nothing. Individual differences, other than opinions of oppressive conservatives, are tolerated and discrimination of other liberals for any reason is not allowed. This is especially true of discrimination based on race, gender or sexual preference. While freedom of the individual is of paramount importance, collective rights of society cannot be infringed. Individual rights must at times be sacrificed for the collective good of all. While the politically correct believe in minimum government interference in individual's lives and freedom and equality for all, a strong central government is necessary to enforce freedom and equality for all citizens.

That there are few, if any, purely politically correct economists is an indictment of the current state of economic and academic elitism in the United States. This is not to say that political correctness has been ignored. Some economists and early philosophers have expressed politically correct ideas but it cannot be said that these thinkers were among the politically correct. After all, political correctness, a manifestation of the enlightened eighties, did not exist as a socially responsible discipline until recently.

The earliest economic theories held that people were responsible for taking care of themselves. They used their limited resources to produce what they needed and no more. People were essentially hunters and gatherers. There was no market to speak of and therefore limited exchange of goods. The basis of distribution was brute force. If your neighbor had gathered or killed something you wanted and if you were big enough and mean enough, you took it. The strong ruled; early economies were command economies. Tradition tended to continue command economies, even until present times. There were and are oppressors and the oppressed. This economic system is unacceptable today, even to the politically incorrect.

Aristotle was one of the first great thinkers to be concerned with the economically oppressed and to express politically correct thought. A crude monetary system had by Aristotle's time been devised to facilitate the exchange of goods and services. It was true then as it is today that economically advantaged oppressors possessed most of the money, which the oppressed would often have to borrow. Aristotle thought that all charges of interest were usurious and saw charging the economically deprived for temporarily using the money of the economically advantaged as a form of oppression. Money, after all, is not productive and has no value in and of itself. Money is valuable only because it is acceptable as a medium of exchange. Money itself does not bring happiness, but as someone once said, I wish I could remember who it was, money enables us to buy a yacht, cruise up to happiness and anchor by it.

Aristotle also felt the market place, as we know it, is unjust. People should produce for themselves, but it was accepted that there would sometimes be surpluses. Producers should sell their surpluses directly to their neighbors at a "just" price. Markets should not be involved. A problem with markets is that they always involve middle humyns who are called marketers. Marketers unjustly gain profit by buying surplus products at a price less than just and selling the same products at a price that is considered more than just. Marketers should be more appropriately called profiteers because they are not responsible for any stage of production and add no value to the products they sell.

Politically correct thought is reflected in the Christian Bible. In the parable of the laborers, narrated by Jesus in the New Testament, workers who came to work late and worked only one hour received the same wages as those who worked a full day. The owner of the vineyard was more interested in the equality of all workers and their welfare than the amount the workers produced. The workers who had worked the full day complained, of course, saying that they had not been treated fairly. The politically incorrect argue that had the parable continued into another day, everyone would have come to work just before quitting time and expected a full days wages. This contention is ridiculous because in a just society,

38

each humyn wants to contribute to the best of his or her ability.

Jeremy Bentham (1748 - 1832) was concerned with achieving and measuring the welfare of society. He believed that welfare could be created only through individual action, but was concerned with society as a whole rather than individuals. If one person loses some welfare, but as a result of this loss another person gains a greater amount of welfare, then society as a whole has benefited. His philosophy reflected the "greatest happiness theory," a term he borrowed from philosophers of the Age of Enlightenment. This simply meant that government and business should produce those things that would provide the greatest happiness for the greatest number of people. He was a prolific writer, but rarely attempted to publish. Upon his death in 1832, he left tens of thousands of pages of unpublished manuscripts and a large sum of money, along with his cadaver, to University College in London. His instructions were that the cadaver be embalmed and prominently displayed at the university. The university administrators were so appreciative that his body still resides in a chair, in a cabinet, in a corridor of the main building at the university.

John Stuart Mill (1806-1873) was an admirer of Bentham's happiness theory and an early believer in using political and social processes to redistribute income. He believed, as the politically correct do today, that economic growth should be sacrificed in order to protect the environment. He also suggested ownership of business by worker-owned cooperatives. He would support achieving equality through a progressive tax system, in which the economically advantaged paid the bulk of the taxes while the oppressed received government-administered benefits. Society should pass other laws to further redistribute wealth. Similarly, he supported equal rights for wimyn and would have been an advocate of the ERA. As evidence of his political correctness, he is reported as saying, "Conservatives are not necessarily stupid, but most stupid people are conservatives."

Thorstein Veblen (1857-1929), an economics professor at the University of Chicago, was extremely critical of the economically advantaged. He saw "conspicuous consumption," the buying of frivolous luxuries just to impress one's neighbors, as a wasteful use of precious resources and inherent in the market place. Since many of Veblen's peers were politically incorrect conspicuous consumers, they saw him as being somewhat differently focused.

Karl Marx (1818-1883) comes closest of all to being a purely politically correct economist. According to Marx, there are two classes of people--the oppressors and the oppressed. The oppressors or capitalists, known as the bourgeoisie, were economically advantaged business owners who continued to enrich themselves through the oppression of the working class, known as the proletariat. According to Marx, if materials to make a product such as a chair cost five dollars and the finished chair sold for twenty dollars, the fifteen-dollar difference is called added value. Marx held that the worker is solely responsible for value added during the process of production. Oppressive capitalist manufacturers would take as profit all value added by workers and in return pay the workers subsistence level wages. The difference between value added, fifteen dollars, and the amount paid to workers, say one dollar, was called surplus value, fourteen dollars, which did nothing but further enrich the already rich economic oppressors. As the economy became more industrialized, capitalists would seek more and more profit. The only way to get more profit was to steal more from the workers, who would soon be making poverty wages. Oppressed workers would eventually become fed up with this arrangement and stage a revolution. After they won the revolution the victorious oppressed workers would establish a "dictatorship of the proletariat" and the state would began to wither away. When the process was completed, a communal system would be established in which all goods belonged to everyone and all humyns were equal. Politically incorrect critics of Marx are quick to point out that a communist revolution has never occurred in a highly industrialized capitalist economy. This does not bother the politically correct because the time for revolutions is not yet right, nor have the right people been fostering the inevitable revolutions.

John Maynard Keynes (1883-1946), exerted more influence on the American economy during the first half of the twentieth century than any other economist since. In *The General Theory of Employment, Interest and Money,* published in 1936, Keynes (pronounced "canes") provided the formula through which the world might extract itself from the Great Depression. He determined that the economic performance of any country was dependent on Aggregate Demand, which was composed of Consumer Spending, Government

Spending, Gross Investment and Net Exports. The magic formula was:

$$AD = C + G + I + X$$

If all of these components were high, the economy would grow. If one or more were low, the economy would go into a slump, a recession or a depression. Ronald Reagan made very clear the difference between the two during a debate with then-president Jimmy Carter in 1980. Reagan said, "When your neighbor loses his job, it' s a recession. When you lose your job, it's a depression." The government cannot control consumers in their spending, business in their investment nor foreigners in their purchases of American goods. Governments do, however, have absolute control of how much money they spend. Keynes therefore advocated that governments spend their way to prosperity. The government can control the economy, eliminating cycles of recession and inflation, through taxing and spending. If economy were in a deep slump, it would be permissible for the government to use deficit spending to provide economic stimulation. This spending could be in the form of government purchases from oppressive businesses or transfers to the economically and motivationally deficient through progressive income taxes. If the economy were plagued by inflation, the government should increase taxes on consumers and businesses to curb their spending and investment, while at the same time reducing its own spending. He believed that government, rather than the market, was responsible for all economic corrections and the economic well being of the nation. It can be said that John Maynard Keynes was the father of modern liberalism, the political and economic philosophy held by the politically correct.

An entire chapter could be written about the ideas of John Kenneth Galbraith, born in 1908. He saw a "dependence effect" in which production created wants. The more people had, the more they wanted, and people would not necessarily want the things that were good for them. He was concerned that large corporations could manipulate markets to ensure their own survival and growth. He was therefore against the free market and, being somewhat of an aristocrat, believed that those of superior minds should determine what is to be produced and what consumers should have. This is consistent with the politically correct position that most people are politically naive and do not know what is good for themselves. Benevolent government regulators can best make those decisions.

There are other economists who would be considered as politically correct but it would be impractical to describe all of them here. There are also many who may be described as politically incorrect. We may say that economists today are of either a conservative (politically incorrect) or liberal (politically correct) philosophy. The difference in the two lies in whether the market or the government should control the economy.

The economizing problem facing all economies is how to answer these three basic questions:

1. What combination of goods and services should be produced?

2. In what quantities should they be produced?

3. For whom are the goods and services produced?

The politically incorrect conservative believes that the market is better equipped to address these questions for three reasons: freedom, incentive to produce and efficiency. Entrepreneurs and workers are free to produce whatever goods they want and work where and when they choose. They are free to further their own self-interests but are also subject to rewards and punishments inherent in the market system. The market provides incentives to produce by allowing individuals to improve their lot in life. Greater work effort means greater income, which results in a higher standard of living.

Finally, the basic argument for the market is that it is efficient. If entrepreneurs want to make substantial business profits they must produce goods that consumers want to buy at a price they can afford to pay. Resources are therefore allocated to produce goods most wanted by society, and lowest-cost production methods are used. Politically incorrect and uninformed conservatives look upon this as allocative and productive efficiency. However, the market system benefits only capitalist oppressors and the economically advantaged. Producers will produce only those goods from which a profit can be made and will produce them in quantities that will maximize profit. Goods and services will be produced only for those who are willing and able to pay for them.

The politically correct economist, liberal in philosophy, is a follower of the economic principles of John Maynard Keynes. H'orsh' believes the government is best suited to answer the basic economizing questions and should implement all economic corrections. The market plays only a minor role, if it plays a role at all. When the market makes decisions such as what is to be produced, in what quantities, and for whom the goods are produced, we find that an inordinate amount of frivolous luxuries are produced for the sole benefit of the economically advantaged. When the government makes production decisions, we find that goods are produced which will benefit the entire population instead of the privileged few. For example, if the government were in charge of all production, there would be no luxury cars or yachts for the fortunate few. Instead, the government would design a car and a boat suitable for all classes and would guarantee that each person had one of each. Distribution would be based on true need instead of ability to pay exorbitant prices administered by profit-driven entrepreneurs.

Economists and sociologists today believe that there are three classes of people--the poor, the middle class and the rich. Yet, for the purpose of income statistics, social economists divide people into five classes of income (quintiles). Current data show that the lower twenty percent of families in the United States receive about five percent of the total income and the highest five percent receive about twenty percent of total income. The distribution of wealth, material possessions and resources is even more depressing. The wealthiest one percent of families own nearly forty percent of all wealth. The bottom twenty percent has to be satisfied with only one-half of one percent of wealth. Such data are useful in measuring the amount of inequality that currently exists in society, and these data indicate that inequality has been steadily increasing over the years.

The politically correct economist believes that there are only two classes of humyns--oppressors and the oppressed. Oppressors are white, male, heterosexual, able-bodied, educated, ambitious, and of sound mind. There are exceptions, of course. Wimyn who are successful at their work, have disavowed feminism and exercise control over others may be considered oppressors. The same is true for independent, successful, educated people of color. The oppressed consists of all others.

Economists of today proclaim that more equality should exist among members of society, yet maintain that inequality is necessary in order to provide incentives to produce. If all were equal, they say, then the opportunity to better oneself would not exist; workers would lose the so-called "American dream" and cease their efforts to attain it. The primary purpose of work, they say, is upward mobility--to move oneself from a lower class to a higher class.

The politically correct economist knows that, since there are only two classes, upward mobility is impossible. The oppressed, consisting of slaves, working humyns, so-called "housewives" and other victims of oppressors, cannot themselves become oppressors. Although the attainment of a single class society in which all are free is desirable and perhaps possible, the politically correct are not naive enough to believe that it is probable. The politically correct economist must develop principles and encourage Congress to pass laws which establish equality of all humyns, constantly instill feelings of guilt in oppressors, and tirelessly work to improve the economic condition of the economically exploited and differently motivated.

But without freedom, equality is meaningless. Freedom of all humyns is necessary in a politically correct economy. Freedom is so important that the politically correct advocate a strong central government to enforce freedom on all members of society.

CH 3: SUPPLY AND DEMAND

Once upon a time an extremely good-looking nonvaginal sexist humyn, visiting from another town, went womynless to a local party attended mostly by local couples. The outward appearance of this visitor was so pleasing to politically incorrect vaginal humyns that one would take him for a famous movie star. He also had that rugged, outdoors look, as though he could have spent some time as a pioneering mountain man in the old west. The party was very elegant with all the local privileged humyns in attendance.

As the movie-star-looking nonvaginal humyn surveyed those in attendance, he was attracted, even fascinated, by a vaginal humyn standing in the corner. He thought she was the most beautiful wofem he had ever seen, even though she had a strange look about her. Her face made one think that she had perhaps in the past had a rather lengthy encounter with a ghost. The look made her even more the temptron.

The stranger felt a stirring in his loins. He wanted her. He *needed* her. He CRAVED her!

Her partner, her significant other, her male sex oppressor, was something entirely different. He was pallid, not particularly attractive, vertically inconvenienced, and appeared to be differently logical. He had the look of one who spent most of his time indoors. He reminded the stranger of one who might have spent considerable time in a job tending bar in a northern city.

The stranger had to have the beautiful-womyn-who-looked-like-she-had-seen-a-ghost. He decided to make his move. After all, in addition to being as handsome as a movie star, he was extremely monetarily privileged. He would make the beautiful wofem and her nonvaginal companion an offer that they would not, could not, resist.

Being malist, the stranger approached the significant other of the beautiful vaginal humyn.

"Sir," he said, "your partner is one of the most beautiful wimyn I have ever seen."

"Thank you," said the beautiful womyn's vertically challenged oppressor. "She is my wife, whom I love very much."

"He means that I am nothing more than an unpaid sex provider, living in his household under legalized incarceration," said the womyn-who-looked-like-she-had-seen-a-ghost.

The stranger spoke again, still to the bar-tender-looking fellow because malist habits are hard to break.

"I would like to be absolutely frank with you. Monetarily speaking, I am extremely well privileged. I have always had everything I have ever wanted. Everything, that is, until now."

The stranger paused, as if to muster his courage and assemble his thoughts.

"I have never had a sex-care provider such as your partner. I am therefore prepared to offer you a proposition. Even though you may think it rather unusual, I make the proposal with the greatest sincerity.

"I would like to offer you, sir, the sum of one million dollars to sleep with your unpaid sex provider for one night."

A thoughtful look, instead of the expected look of shock, came over the face of the handsomely deficient young nonvaginal humyn.

"It just so happens that things have not been good for us lately. You might say that we are currently cash-flow challenged. Your proposal is somewhat interesting to me, but the final decision must be left to my partner. Would you excuse us for a few minutes?"

The couple moved to another corner of the room and appeared to be having a serious conversation. In a few moments they returned. It was now the vaginal humyn who did the speaking.

"Sir, because at the time we are economically challenged, we have decided to accept your proposal, *indecent* though it may be. Does tonight suit your schedule?"

The handsome stranger seemed to become a little nervous. He looked at his feet, which began a sort of subtle shuffle. A few beads of sweat formed on the end of his nose. His bottom lip began to flutter nervously.

"It seems that I, too, have a slight but temporary cash-flow deficiency," the stranger said.

"The truth is, I don't have a million dollars on me at the time. Would you consider taking twenty dollars?"

The homely-deficient young womyn looked extremely shocked. "WHAT DO YOU THINK I AM?" she shouted.

"That has already been established," said the handsome stranger. "We are now haggling over price!"

(My apologies to Mark Twain, the motion picture industry and others for the above story)

The point is that what the beautiful young womyn was willing and able to sell for one million dollars, she was either unwilling or unable to sell for twenty!

What the handsome young stranger was probably willing but unable to buy for one million dollars, he was more than willing, and certainly able, to pay twenty bucks!

These are the laws of supply and demand, upon which the capitalist economic system is based.

Supply is the propensity to sell. The law of supply says that we will be willing and able to sell more of any item at higher prices. It also means that things we would not be willing to part with at a low price, we will gladly sell if the price is right. The following illustrates supply and the law of supply of Dilly Boppers:

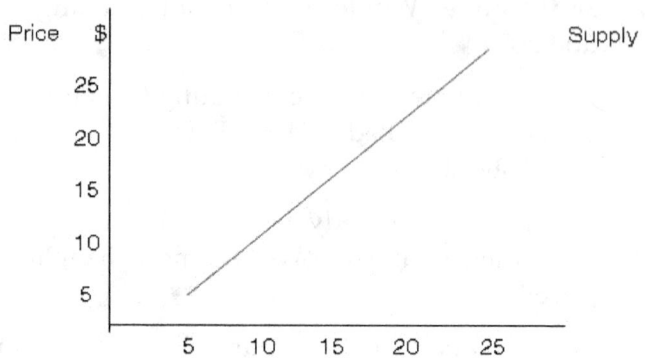

Price $ Supply

25

20

15

10

5

      5   10   15   20   25

The graph clearly shows that producers are willing and able to produce more Dilly Boppers at higher prices than at lower prices. The reasoning behind this should be obvious. The more that can be sold at higher prices, the more profit can be made.

It is the belief of capitalist oppressors that every humyn, acting under the role of self-interest and in compliance with the law of supply, has a price at which h'orsh' will sell themselves, their souls, the family jewels, the homestead or any other heirloom of formerly immeasurable value. Humyns have been known to sell even one another, as tribes in Africa once did when, during the various stages of tribal warfare, members of victorious tribes sold survivors of losing tribes into slavery.

Before the days of political correctness, when unpaid sex workers were called wives and male sex oppressors were called husbands, society believed in an abstract emotion called "love." The state of "being in love" was blamed for all sorts of aberrant social and sexual behavior of all species of animality, both vaginal and nonvaginal.

A "wife" of those days would be sitting at the dinner table with her "husband" (one of the aberrant behaviors was family units having their meals together, all at one time). The vaginal humyn might say something like, "Darling, I love you so much that I wouldn't take a million dollars for you." According to the law of supply, the reason that he had not been sold is that the "wife" had not yet received an appropriate offer. The politically correct suspect that, with an offer considerably less than the stated million dollars, the unpaid sex worker would have gladly and quickly shed herself of the legalized rapist. In many cases, assuming that she has sufficient economic empowerment, the politically correct hufem would pay nearly that amount to anyone who would take the amore deficient, motivationally challenged male oppressor off her hands.

The new politically astute also understand that the law of supply provides proof that the often-made statement by the goal-oriented white male oppressor politician that, "I am an honorable man. I cannot be bought," is truth deficient when profit is an incentive.

Demand is the propensity to buy and, like supply, is a necessary component of the capitalist market system. No matter how badly a supplier wants to sell an item, there must be someone who is willing and able to buy if a transaction is to be consummated.

The law of demand states that humyns are willing and able to buy more goods at lower prices than at higher prices. Again, one must be both willing and able to purchase the goods. The law of demand therefore leads to further oppression because the economically challenged will be unable to purchase the expensive goods and services so cherished by the rich. However, even the economically disadvantaged and differently motivated would be quite willing to buy such frivolous luxuries if they had proper economic empowerment.

Elitist economists justify the existence of the law of demand in several ways. One reason given is that it makes sense. As a converse to the law of supply, it is the nature of humyns to buy something if they think they are getting it at a cheap enough price, generally less than it's worth. Humyns, especially capitalist male oppressors, enjoy cheating others out of their worldly possessions whenever possible. Consumers can also afford to purchase more at lower prices.

The following graph shows demand and the law of demand. This graph is down slopping, showing an inverse relation between price and quantity demanded.

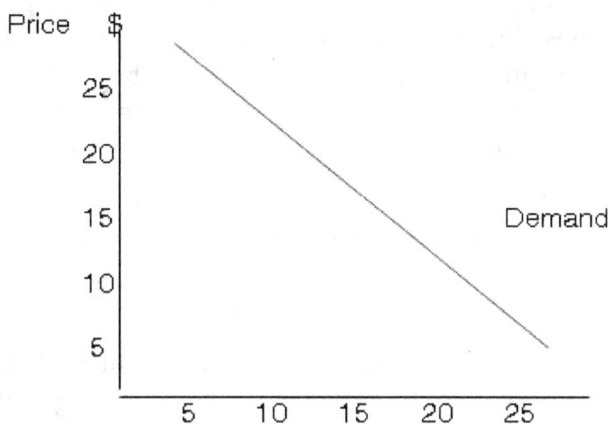

The graph shows that consumers will be willing and able to buy twenty-five Dilly Boppers at five dollars but will buy only five at twenty-five dollars.

Another capitalistic justification for the law of demand is an abstract concept called the law of diminishing marginal utility. Remember that in economics, utility means satisfaction and margin means change. Marginal utility means additional satisfaction associated with additional consumption. This concept is so important that an entire chapter will be dedicated to the subject. For the present, it is necessary to know only that less additional satisfaction is derived from each additional unit of anything that is consumed. Since we get less satisfaction from each additional unit, we are not as willing to pay as much for subsequent units as we were previous units.

Higher levels of satisfaction from each additional unit consumed, as is sometimes the case with frivolous luxuries, leads to higher prices. Only economically advantaged oppressors can afford those things that provide a large amount of marginal utility and therefore the rich receive greater satisfaction from life than the disadvantaged.

Politically correct economists see another, deeper meaning in the concept of marginal utility. It is obviously a major statement against inequality. This is the subject of a later chapter.

With the capitalistic market acting under the laws of supply and demand, sales of goods and services can occur only when buyers and sellers agree on price. Sellers must be willing and able to take the price buyers are willing and able to pay. This is called the market price, or equilibrium price. If prices are lower than market price, more will be demanded than is supplied, resulting in a shortage of the item. If prices are higher than market price, more will be supplied than is demanded. There will then be a surplus of the subject item. Only at market price will there be neither a surplus nor a shortage.

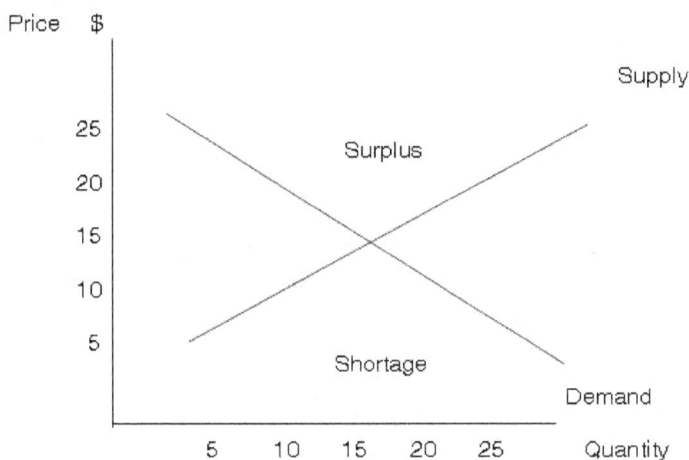

The graph shows that the equilibrium (or market) price of Dilly Boppers is fifteen dollars. If the price is five dollars, only five will be produced but twenty-five will be demanded. A shortage will occur and the price will be driven up. At a price of twenty-five dollars, twenty-five Dilly Boppers will be produced but only five will be sold. A surplus of twenty will occur and the price of Dilly Boppers will be driven down. Only at a price of fifteen dollars will the quantity demanded equal the quantity supplied.The politically correct economist sees the capitalistic market with its laws of supply and demand and equilibrium prices as particularly mean-spirited. The economically challenged cannot pay the prices that industrialist oppressors want for their products. Furthermore, because capitalist oppressors have monopolistic power, they do not lower prices so that products providing high marginal utility will be within the price range of the economically challenged. Rich oppressors therefore make products for one another. They are both suppliers and demanders.

The capitalistic economic system will not be fair and just until governments ensure that adequate provisions are made for the economically exploited and the motivationally deficient. The current market system, based upon supply and demand, equilibrium prices and equilibrium quantities, leads to increasing inequality. When all humyns are equal, the incentives of price and profit will disappear. The economy will then not waste precious resources producing frivolous luxuries for the economically advantaged. Only those goods that provide an equal amount of pleasure to each humyn will be produced.

The politically correct call upon Congress to repeal the laws of supply and demand!

Ch 4 : THE STORY OF MONEY AND BANKING

Money is described in the Christian Bible as something the love of which is the root of all evil. Yet, one of the points on which nearly all economists agree is that money, in and of itself, is worthless. Money has no intrinsic value. Why is it, then, that humyns regularly abuse or kill other humyns for money? How can so many people desire something that elitist economists declare as worthless?

The answer, say economists, is that while money does not provide any direct satisfaction, it allows humyns to acquire those goods that do provide satisfaction.

Money is valuable only because of its acceptability in exchange for goods and services. When money is no longer acceptable, it no longer has value. It therefore stands to reason that anything that society accepts in exchange for goods and services can be money. Indeed, many things have been used as money in this country. Early Native Americans used wampum, beads of polished shells strung in strands or belts, as their medium of exchange. Early oppressors of Western Native Americans would exchange horses with Native American chiefs for a vaginal humyn to serve as an unpaid sex worker throughout the long, cold winters. The white oppressors of the era would also exchange for their winter provisions the skins of nonhumyn animals that they had assassinated during the summer months. Vaginal humyns have even been known to exchange sex for items that provide various amounts of satisfaction.

In the ultimate oppression of Native Americans, the ethically challenged European male cheated the rightful owners out of Manhattan Island for a mere twenty-four dollars in trinkets, beads and baubles.

Beads, horses, nonhumyn animal skins, sex, and trinkets and baubles were used as commodity money in the above examples, but such commodities may not be acceptable in other times and under other conditions. The politically correct would certainly not accept the skins of nonhumyn animals in exchange for goods. Nor would they be involved in the trading of nonvaginal humyns. Religious conservatives would probably object to sex as commodity money. Something had to be used as money that would be acceptable to all. The answer is fiat money.

Fiat money is money because the government says it is, and is therefore a type of funny money. It is not backed by anything of value, which is the major difference between fiat money and commodity money. Commodity money can provide direct satisfaction. The malist Native Americans who traded the vaginal humyns of their communes to white European oppressors derived pleasure from riding their newly acquired horses. Recipients of the nonhumyn animal skins derived

60

mentally deficient pleasure from wearing the skins as furs. Trinkets and baubles were worn as beads. Fiat money provides satisfaction only when it is exchanged for something of value.

Money has four basic uses in any economy. (Some economists say there are only three uses, so we see that this is another matter in which elitist economists disagree.) Perhaps the most important use of money is as a medium of exchange. This is certainly the best-known and most common use.

Another use is as a standard of value. A monetary unit familiar to all allows sellers to place prices on their respective goods and services. If the price of a loaf of bread is $2.30, then the seller thinks the bread is "worth" $2.30. The buyer must agree that the bread is worth that amount before making the purchase. Worth is therefore a matter of personal opinion.

A third use of money is as a store of value. The economically privileged keep money in their checking accounts, foreign banks and other safe shelters for emergency use. Economic oppressors also invest in large amounts of foreign currency in order to protect themselves against the declining American dollar. The economically oppressed are generally satisfied with keeping their meager savings in Mason jars hidden around their homes or buried in their yards.

The fourth use of money, and this is the one upon which some economists disagree, is as a standard of deferred payments. Money provides a convenient measure of how much one owes, and how much one must save in the future in order to make the required payments on debt.

One cannot speak of money without considering the ultimate institution of oppression of the economically challenged--the commercial bank. Banks evolved from the practices of ancient goldsmiths and are a creation of European white males for their descendants.

Suppose, during the days of the mythical oppressor monarch King Arthur, a knight should arrive in a strange town on his companion animal, which is engaged at the time in providing personal transport. The purpose of the visit is to acquire a castle for his soon-to-be unpaid sex provider. Since knights were malist and sexist, he continued to refer to her as his future wife.

Knights of the day were generally economically privileged and this knight was especially so. He had several pieces of gold in his possession, the bulk of which was for the purpose of buying the castle. Another indication of the degree of sexual oppression of the day is that the knight did not allow his future partner to share in the decision of which castle to purchase. Indeed, the castle-buying decision should have been the decision of the womyn alone since it would be she who would maintain the interior of the castle while the knight was off on his crusades or slaying dragons.

A problem of the day, as it still is in modern times, was to find a safe place in which to keep one's gold while visiting unfamiliar places. Even in those days of chivalry it was not uncommon for a black knight to knock a white knight in the head and take his possessions. A solution was provided by the local goldsmith. People have always placed a high value on gold and have desired luxurious baubles made of the metal, frivolous though they may be. Malist oppressors who were seeking favors often gave gold baubles to vaginal humyns. For that matter, they still do. Gold was valued so highly that those who believed in the brute force method of distribution often attempted to steal the gold of other humyns. The goldsmith would therefore have a safe place, or strong room, in which to keep his gold. Local goldsmiths would gladly store safely the gold of visitors of economic substance while they were in town. Of course, an appropriate fee would be assessed for the service.

In storing gold for the visiting knight, the goldsmith had initiated a service now provided by all commercial banks--holding the deposits of rich, white European oppressors and their descendants.

Then, as now, most humyns engaged in brokering real estate were vaginal. The knight would meet with the hufem engaged in brokering real property in the early hours of the first morning in town. She would show the knight several less than appealing castles first, saving the best offering for later in the day. As soon as the knight saw this castle, he knew it was the one that he wanted for his future domestically incarcerated vaginal humyn.

"My future wife (remember that the knight was not yet politically enlightened) will love this castle," said the knight. "How much is it?"

"Ten pieces of gold," replied the real estate salesfem.

"That's exactly the amount I have in the goldsmith's strong room," said the knight. (The wofem knew how much gold the knight had, because she and the goldsmith are mutual sex care providers. She had extracted information about the knight the previous evening by temporarily employing a maneuver military strategists call a withholding action.) "I will need at least one piece for my trip home. (The knight actually had two pieces of gold hidden in his boot. The buyer and seller of real estate thus established a tradition of mutual lying that continues today.) Besides, this castle is not in perfect repair. It looks like it needs a new roof."

"The roof is in perfect condition," said the real estate salesfem, thus continuing the newly established tradition. "I also have another buyer waiting to see this castle later this evening. If you don't want to buy it, I am sure the other party will." (This statement was also truth deficient.)

"I had better buy it, then," conceded the knight. "We can go to the goldsmith's store and I can get the gold for you."

It was very late in the day by this time and the goldsmith was closed. He was at home preparing his chamber for an expected visit from the real estate wofem.

"I guess we will have to wait until tomorrow," said the knight. "I really wanted to finish this tonight so I could get an early start home in the morning."

The real estate wofem also wanted to close the sale as soon as possible. In addition to a developing vaginal ache as she thought of the goldsmith, she was fearful that if the closing were delayed until

64

the morrow the knight might find a castle better to his liking through a competing castle broker.

"I know what we can do," said the wofem. "The goldsmith knows me quite well. When you left your gold in his safekeeping, he gave you a receipt for exactly ten pieces. That's the price of the castle! You can give me the receipt and I will pick the gold up tomorrow. We can sign the paperwork now and you can be on your way early in the morning!" The deal was thus consummated.

The castle was paid for not with gold, but with worthless pieces of paper representing gold. Soon people would trade gold receipts for various products and services as they previously traded pieces of gold. In order to save time and be ready for increasing numbers of depositors, goldsmiths began to preprint receipts that were symbolic of one piece of gold. When a citizen brought gold to the goldsmith for safekeeping, the goldsmith would give the depositor one piece of paper for each piece of gold. The goldsmith had inadvertently invented paper money, backed by gold!

Now we can move forward to some later, undetermined time. Another knight is in town to buy a castle for his significant other. This knight had also left his gold in the care of the goldsmith and had received twelve pieces of paper as receipts for his twelve pieces of gold. He was shown a castle by the real estate salesfem, a castle that he thought would be to the liking of his unpaid sex provider.

The knight inquired, "What is the asking price of this castle?"

"A mere eleven pieces of gold," replied the salesfem. (This was a period of moderate inflation.) "The price is firm," she added.

"I suppose I will take it," said the knight. "But my gold is at the goldsmith's. Since it is late, we shall have to wait until the morning to close."

"I don't think so," said the salesfem. "You may just give me the receipts for eleven of the twelve pieces of gold you have." (*OOPS*, she thought. *The knight would know that she was getting inside information from the goldsmith. How else would she know that the knight actually had twelve pieces of gold?*)

However, the knight was gray-matter challenged and did not notice the realfem's slip-of-the-tongue.

"That is quite impossible," said the knight. "Thieves seem to be stealing the receipts as they were stealing gold. I left them in the safe at the Knights Inn. I can't retrieve them until morning."

Again, for reasons stated previously, the salesfem did not want to delay the closing until morning.

"I'm afraid it may not be available by then," she said. "There is someone just around the bend of the road who wants me to show them this castle as soon as we are finished. This castle won't last long. You had better think of something."

"I know what might work," said the knight. I have known the goldsmith for a few months and he knows my signature. I will just take my lunch bag and write a message telling him to pay you the amount of eleven pieces of gold. He will recognize my signature and turn the gold over to you."

Through another inadvertent happenstance of fate, the check was born.

A few months later another knight came through town. This knight was in town on business other than buying a castle, but happened to encounter the real estate salesfem in the lounge of the Knights Inn. During their conversation, she told him of an excellent deal on a castle she had listed. "If you are even thinking about getting into the market," she said, "you had better look into this. At only twelve pieces of gold (inflation again), it won't last long."

The knight still wasn't convinced, but after being exposed to the wofem's fuzzy persuader a few times in the knight's room later that evening, he decided that it would at least be worth an hour or so of his time to see the castle.

He did in fact like the castle. He thought that if he ever had a significant other, she would like the castle also. During the interim it might be nice to have a place such as this to come on weekends. After all, the real estate wofem seemed to not have a significant other and her persuader was indeed a powerful and memorable tool.

"I would like to buy the castle," said the knight, "but alas, I did not bring any gold."

This was extremely disappointing to the real estate salesfem. She wanted very much for the knight to purchase the castle and had even considered lowering the price. The goldsmith had, at least temporarily, become an insignificant other and the knight had the previous evening proved to be a more than adequate substitute sex provider.

She said, "I shall see what I can do."

She returned to her office and arranged an assignation with the goldsmith. She knew that the fuzzy persuader possessed by all females was a powerful weapon when properly employed, and would be instrumental in the eventual domination of sexist male oppressors by enlightened feminists. By midevening, the goldsmith would be more then ready to offer assistance to the traveling knight.

"You see," said the goldsmith to the knight the next morning, "I have all this gold here that I have stored for people in this town. Nobody ever picks any of it up, or they don't pick up much of it, anyway. The total amount I have on hand never decreases by more than ten percent. I figure that if I keep on hand only twenty percent of all the gold I have deposited, I will have more than enough to take care of my customers' gold needs. I can easily let you use twelve pieces of gold to buy the castle. You must promise me in writing, however, that you will return the twelve pieces of gold, plus one more piece for my trouble, to me within six months."

The goldsmith therefore created the fractional reserve system used by banks the world over and the lending of those reserves. Banks no longer are required to keep all their deposits in the vault. They need to keep only enough money on hand to take care of day-to-day transactions. It is this feature, however, that resulted in many banks having to close their doors during the first days of the Great Depression. There was not enough money on hand when panic-stricken depositors, fearful of losing their life's savings, made runs on their local banks to withdraw their deposits.

But that was not all the goldsmith did. "There is no need for me to burden you with heavy gold," said the goldsmith. "I will just give you some of these gold receipts. People are trading them just like gold, and I have preprinted them as "pay to the bearer" in denominations of one and five pieces of gold. I have only 1,000 pieces of gold on deposit and have extra receipts."

When the goldsmith gave the knight the twelve receipts, there were now 1,012 receipts in circulation. *The goldsmith had actually created money representing twelve pieces of gold by lending his excess reserves. By excess reserves, we mean the pieces of gold that the goldsmith did not expect his customers to pick up.* The real estate salesfem accepted the receipts as readily as she would gold, for she knew they would be accepted in trade for service at the local tavern.

It doesn't matter that there was no gold to back up the twelve new receipts; it was still money because it could be traded for various goods in the economy. When the knight brought twelve pieces of gold to the goldsmith to repay the loan, the money would be decreased.

Commercial banks create money today by lending their excess reserves. Since lending creates money, the target of money creation is the borrower. Because of our oppressive banking system, humyns must have collateral in order to borrow money. Using their existing factories as collateral, rich capitalists borrow money to build more factories in which the poor and oppressed work, but workers cannot borrow money because they have no collateral. They therefore remain oppressed workers. As the goldsmith created money for rich knights of the middle ages, commercial banks of today create money for rich descendants of dead white European male oppressors.

CH 5: THE AMERICAN BANKING SYSTEM

As noted in the previous chapter, money is the source of all evil. Of all the social inventions of dead white European male oppressors and their descendants, money is by far the most insidious. It is the leading cause of crime throughout the world. Brothers kill brothers. Neighbors kill neighbors. Homes are invaded by criminals. Foreign countries are invaded by other countries. Parents sell their daughters into prostitution. Brothers sell brothers into slavery. Vaginal humyns prostitute themselves.

All for money.

The Bible, held in reverence and unquestioned belief by religious denominations throughout the world, describes and even sanctions the use of money for the oppression of the masses by the privileged.

The book of Genesis describes how Abraham is told by God in their covenant that all males in his house *including those bought with money*, oppressed humyns known as slaves, should be circumcised. In the Book of Ecclesiastics, readers of the Bible are told that money answers all things.

Finally in the New Testament, some form of economic and political correctness begins to emerge. It is here that Paul, in his first epistle to Timothy, describes money, or the love of it, as being the root of all evil. In the parable of the laborers, contained in the twentieth chapter of Matthew, the wealthy but politically correct landowner paid the workers who came to work only an hour before quitting time the same wages as those who worked all day. The politically incorrect would say that all workers would show up for work the next day one hour before quitting time and expect a full days wages.

For all the trouble it has caused, money would without a doubt seem to be the most valuable invention of humynkind. Yet, according to elitist economists, money in and of itself has no value at all! Money provides no direct satisfaction and is worth only what it can buy. Therein lie its oppressive characteristics. In order to buy something it is necessary to have money. In the economy of the United States, only oppressive capitalists and the economically advantaged have enough money to purchase frivolous luxuries desired by all humyns. Money is therefore the primary cause of inequality and the tool used by oppressors to keep the oppressed in their places.

Three broad types of money are, or have been, in use. The first is full-value commodity currency, in which the value of the money is the same as the value of the commodity. The most familiar of this type is *specie*, which generally consists of gold and silver coins, and was the favorite of the original white Eurocentric oppressors. However, anything that has value can be used as commodity money.

Displaced white European males of the early West, called mountain male humyns, routinely acquired Native American vaginal humyns to provide sex and warmth during the long winters. Chiefs of the Native American tribes were quite willing to accept horses in exchange for the wofems. Anything can be commodity money as long as it has value and is acceptable in exchange for various goods. The major problem with this category of money is that if one is to become richer, then more of the valuable commodity must be gathered. It is unlikely that economic oppressors would take the commodity from each other so they would confiscate what little of the commodity the economically oppressed still owned. Another problem is that commodities such as grain or horses either spoil or die.

The second type of money is full-value representative money. The value of this money is still based on some sort of commodity, but something other than the actual commodity is used in the exchange process. Pieces of paper are usually used, after being certified by some recognized authority, to represent the commodity. Examples are the receipts for gold printed by the goldsmiths in the previous chapter. More recent examples are gold certificates and silver certificates issued by the United States Government in the late 1800s and early 1900s.

However, the major problem still exists. In order to have more money, one must own, or have control of, more of the commodity.

In both cases, full-value commodity money and full-value representative money, it is sometimes difficult for the oppressors to further increase their riches. Commodities often occur in fixed quantities. If not fixed, their quantities are at least limited and difficult to acquire. Once enough paper currency is printed to represent the total value of gold, silver, or whatever commodity is used as the standard, then no more money can be created. The acquisition of wealth then becomes a zero-sum activity. One rich oppressor can gain riches only at the expense of another, with the gains of one and the losses of another summing to zero. In an ideal politically incorrect world, all oppressors should increase their riches simultaneously. This is extremely difficult to do because there is only a limited amount of full-value money. Another type of money was therefore necessary.

The third type of money, created solely for the benefit of wealthy oppressors, is credit money, often called fiat money. It is money only because the government says it is money, and has no intrinsic value. Further, it does not represent anything of value. Credit money, in and of itself, is absolutely valueless. What can credit money consist of? Anything, as long as the government says it is money, but it is usually pieces of paper or coins with no intrinsic value.

While money is the instrument of oppression, the United States banking system is the institution of its administration.

Simply stated, credit money is created through bookkeeping entries when banks lend money they don't have, much as the goldsmith did when excess gold receipts were lent to the knight to buy the castle, thus "creating" new money. Because of this money-creating loan transaction, the vast majority

74

of money in the United States is "credit money." Credit money is money for the wealthy since only they can qualify for loans, especially larger loans such as mortgage loans and loans for luxury cars, boats and the like. Since the economically marginalized cannot qualify for loans necessary to purchase these goods, they are denied the money needed to buy such luxuries.

Money is therefore the leading cause of inequality.

It is no wonder. The Federal Reserve System controls the United States banking system, which creates money by lending. The Federal Reserve System is commonly referred to as "The Fed."

In the summer of 1907, the American economy entered a slump as many businesses and Wall Street brokerage houses went bankrupt. Stock market prices fell and depositors made a run on the nation's banks. Much of the nation's money, consisting of bank notes issued by individual banks, became worthless. Even bank notes issued by solvent banks were suspect because no one knew which banks could back their notes. The United States was on the verge of a barter economy. The need for reform to bring about soundness to the American banking system led to the passing of the Federal Reserve Act of 1913, establishing for the third time a national bank of the United States. Congress for a variety of demographic and political reasons did not renew the first two.

The purpose of a national bank, or Federal Reserve System as proposed in Congress by William Jennings Bryan, acting as chief lieutenant for President Woodrow Wilson, and implemented by Senator Robert Owen of Oklahoma and Representative Carter Glass of Virginia, was to establish policies which would eliminate problems caused by boom and bust cycles. Such cycles result from using the standard of gold as a basis for the monetary system. In order for a gold-based system to work, the price of gold and hence the value of money must be immune from cycles of inflation and deflation. Since gold is a commodity, this is nearly impossible. President Wilson wanted a system that would benefit both the economically disadvantaged and economically advantaged alike, calling for those governing the Federal banking system to be representative of the general public interest in the Federal reserve district and be immune from party politics.

The Senate, being more interested in the welfare of the economically advantaged than the economically disadvantaged, had other ideas. They were heavily influenced by a white Eurocentric oppressive German immigrant named Paul Moritz Warburg. Warburg had worked in Germany in the family business, the M. M. Warburg Company, administering the Rothschild Fund. The Rothschild fund would later finance Kaiser Wilhelm's war against the United States and, strangely, the war of the United States against Germany, and the Russian revolution. In the meantime, the Rothschilds wanted to make sure that their banking firms did not lose any of their influence and control over the American monetary system during any monetary reform movements. To this end, Warburg was installed as a partner in the banking firm of Kuhn, Loeb and Company.

76

The process through which the Fed was created is somewhat of a mystery. Following the panic of 1907, Senator Nelson Aldrich, one of the most powerful men in Congress and father-in-law of John D. Rockefeller, Jr. proposed the National Currency Act. This act led to creation of the National Monetary Commission, headed by Senator Aldrich and a prelude to the Federal Reserve System. In 1910, Aldrich called a meeting of the Monetary Commission and oppressive bankers at a hunting lodge on Jekyll Island, Georgia. Presumed to be on a duck-hunting expedition, those attending were sworn to secrecy and not allowed to leave or communicate with anyone outside the hunting lodge. They addressed each other by code names during meetings. Those in attendance included the most powerful banking and political names in the country, including Warburg, J. P. Morgan, John D. Rockefeller and Bernard Baruch. After ten days, they emerged with the rudiments of the Federal Reserve System. They and their oppressive banking associates would be its primary benefactors. Still, no one knows exactly what went on at the Jekyll Island meeting.

The debate over the Federal Reserve Act then became a power struggle between those who would support the economically and motivationally deficient and those who supported the oppressive banking powers of the day, represented as always by the United States Senate. It was no contest. The requirement that those governing the Federal Reserve Banks be "representative of the general public interest" was replaced by the phrase that they be "persons of tested banking experience." This effectively placed the control of all future credit money in the hands of large international banking firms, servants of rich, white, Eurocentric oppressors the world over.

`The Fed, the central bank of the United States, consists of twelve regional banks; a Board of Governors, led for years under both Democratic and Republican presidents by the now retired bipartisan oppressor Alan Greenspan; the Federal Open Market Committee and an Advisory Committee. The Board of Governors consists of seven members, appointed by the President of the United States for terms of 14 years, arranged so that the term of one expires every even-numbered year. Members are supposedly apolitical, swearing allegiance to neither the Republican or Democratic Party nor the president who appointed her or him. The job of the Board of Governors is to set broad monetary policy.

The Advisory Committee is composed of about twenty prominent oppressors such as bankers, economists, college professors and university presidents. The job of the Advisory Committee is to advise the Board of Governors, advice that may or may not be heeded.

The Federal Open Market Committee, consisting of the seven members of the Board of Governors and select presidents of the Federal Reserve District Banks, is by far the most oppressive group in the Fed. This committee is charged with the task of controlling interest rates and in turn the money supply. They are called the Open Market Committee because one of the primary tools used to control the money supply is open market operations--the buying and selling of government bonds. If the FOMC wants to decrease the money supply, they simply offer more government bonds for sale, often at rather lucrative interest rates. Money used to pay for the bonds is taken out of circulation, decreasing the money supply. This shortage of money drives interest rates even higher. This is seen by the politically correct as particularly mean-spirited because the economically deficient and motivationally dispossessed cannot now afford even the necessities of life such as new cars and middle-class homes because they cannot afford to pay the high finance charges.

If the money supply is to be increased, the FOMC does just the opposite. They buy back government bonds, often at premium prices that further enrich their fellow oppressors. The new money in circulation now tends to drive interest rates down.

Another tool used by the FOMC is the discount interest rate, which is the rate at which the Fed lends its member banks money. When discount rates are lowered, oppressive bankers can borrow money from their reserve bank more cheaply and lend it at lower interest rates. Member banks place the money in circulation through loans to their favored depositors. The economically marginalized are more willing to borrow money at the lower interest rates and now can afford to purchase a few of the necessities of life.

A lower discount rate also allows banks to create more money themselves. As you will recall from the previous chapter, it is a peculiarity of the American banking system, and banking systems everywhere, that when money is lent, money is also created. No actual money is involved in the loan transaction. Money is lent by making two entries in the bank's ledgers. Assume a loan for one thousand dollars. An entry-- $1,000-- is made in the borrower's demand deposit (checking) account. This is a liability to the bank. Another entry is made in the bank's accounts receivable--$1,000--a loan that is an asset to the bank and keeps the books balanced in the double-entry bookkeeping system. Through these two transactions, one thousand dollars in brand new money is created. It is obvious that some control must be exercised over this ability of banks to create money through lending. The Fed does this by controlling interest rates.

Lower interest rates provide some benefit to the middle class, but they never get low enough to allow the economically oppressed to buy new cars, boats, recreational vehicles and other expensive consumer goods; they merely spend the newly created money buying necessities of life from capitalists. Lower rates allow white male oppressive bank owners to further enrich themselves through the usurious practice of borrowing at low rates and lending at higher rates.

When discount rates are increased, just the opposite happens. Fewer and fewer people can afford to borrow money and less "new" money is created. This is especially punishing to the economically depressed because at the new ultra-usurious interest rates, they cannot now afford to borrow money to obtain even the necessities of life.

It should be noted that nearly all state legislatures, controlled by representatives of the banking industry and lawyers, have over the past few years repealed or drastically changed their usury laws which protect the economically marginalized from oppressive interest rates. Consumer finance or "revolving charge accounts" used by consumer finance companies and major department stores when selling the necessities of life to the poor and oppressed are not subject to usury laws.

It is the claim of the Fed that the purpose of controlling the money supply is to eliminate the damaging cycles of economic enrichment and negative economic growth. However, there is a collateral effect, which provides great benefit to economically enhanced investors and members of the banking establishment. Inflation occurs as the money supply increases. During periods of inflation, money losses some of its value. Each dollar owned by financial oppressors and the oppressed alike is worth less. Prices are driven up. Oppressive capitalist merchants can then sell their goods and property at these inflated prices, making even more obscene profits. The reaction of the Fed is to drive interest rates up, allowing oppressive bankers to lend money at even higher interest rates. Since interest rate is the price of money, the oppressed must now pay exorbitant prices in order to borrow money to obtain the bare necessities, which because of inflation are also at exorbitant prices,

There will then occur a period of economic adjustment during which a recession is likely. Oppressed workers will be released from their jobs.

The unfortunate unemployed oppressed, who can no longer make their mortgage payments or the monthly car payment, will be forced to sell their property to capitalists or oppressive banks will repossess it. Interest rates are now driven down, more money will be created and prices will decrease. Capitalist oppressors purchase property from the economically oppressed at bargain basement prices. The economically privileged can now borrow money at low interest rates to further increase their investment holdings.

During the subsequent cycle of inflation, oppressors may sell property back to the economically marginalized at the resulting higher prices. The disadvantaged will again be forced to mortgage their futures to oppressive bankers.

It is obvious to the politically correct that the current monetary system of the United States is the servant of the rich and must undergo major revision.

A major problem associated with the current United States monetary system is that it is unconstitutional. Article One of the Constitution states that *The Congress shall have the power to coin money, regulate the value thereof...* In spite of this clearly stated provision, the Federal Reserve Banks create money, issue paper money and then regulate the value of money by setting interest rates (that is, setting the price of money and regulating its value). This power should be returned to Congress, specifically the House of Representatives. As the name indicates, they are the true representatives of economically marginalized people. To fairly regulate the value of money would be an impossible task for the members of the Senate since their primary concern is the welfare of the economically privileged.

It should be pointed out that fair regulation of the value of money could also be a problem in the House of Representatives. During the second Clinton administration and the administration of the illegally appointed George W. Bush, Republicans held a majority of House seats. Republicans are representatives of the economically advantaged and will bias their regulation in favor of oppressive capitalists. While it may be impossible to get rid of all Republicans as some of the more astute politically correct have recommended, Republicans are particularly mean-spirited and some way must be found to limit their representation in Congress. The time may be right for a Constitutional amendment that addresses that very problem.

The United Sates Constitution is a living document that must be open to change. Only liberals, comprising the bulk of the membership of the Democrat Party, support change. The enlightened correct, both politically and economically, support a Constitutional Amendment limiting the number of conservatives in Congress to a minority, therefore providing for correct interpretation and amending of the current Constitution. At the time there is a good chance that such an amendment would receive the necessary votes. But time is short. The amendment must be passed with haste because more and more Democrats are becoming turncoats and joining the Republican Party. Even more are becoming disloyal by voting for Republican candidates while remaining members of the Democratic Party. This has come about primarily because of emotional arguments offered daily on radio talk shows by ultraconservative and simple-minded hosts.

Whatever the method, the power to regulate the value of money must be taken from the Fed, an agency that is a servant of male white oppressors and is independent of Congressional oversight. The power must be returned to the people through a Congress that represents the economically challenged.

An alternative solution would be to do away with our current monetary system entirely. A new system would be developed in which vouchers, such as food stamps and Medicaid certificates currently in use, would be used to exchange for goods and services. Under this system, a family would be allotted a predetermined amount of food for each member, and only food could be obtained with a food voucher. This would ensure that money to buy milk for the baby would not be spent buying lottery tickets as is currently being done. Indeed, the government could ensure milk for babies by issuing families with small children vouchers for milk only. For the most part, to allow choice of menus, families would be given vouchers that would allow them to buy any combination of food types they desire. However, it may be necessary at times to issue vouchers that are good only for seldom purchased items such as liver and broccoli to ensure that families eat healthy food.

Such a system could provide the government an opportunity to bring to a halt the needless slaughter of nonhumyn animals by refusing to issue vouchers for the purchase of meat.

An important collateral benefit to the food voucher system is one of health. The government could control obesity by issuing fewer food vouchers to those determined by an appropriate committee to possess an alternative body image.

Vouchers would be issued for clothes, cars, utilities, home entertainment electronics, companion animals, items of personal hygiene and even limited cosmetics. That's the major advantage of voucher money. The government could make certain that each humyn and nonhumyn animal receives everything that h'orsh'it needs. There would be no inequality since the needs for all are determined provided by a benevolent government.

It would also lead to economic efficiency. No frivolous luxuries would be produced under a voucher monetary system. There would not be Cadillacs, Lincoln Continentals and Ford Mustangs. Congress would finally design a car that would suit all. There would be no difference in suits purchased at Brooks Brothers or at J. C. Penney's. All suits would be the same and obtained only with a new-suit voucher. Malist egos would be placed in proper perspective.

It is to be expected that the current group of white male oppressors will resist with vigor the transition to voucher money. But that is not the concern of the politically correct. Complete equality and the end of oppression is the ultimate goal. No one is free as long as oppression exists. Freedom and oppression cannot coexist.

CH.6: MARGINAL UTILITY

A brief discussion of marginal utility is necessary to provide justification for equality of all humyns and elimination of the economically privileged classes.

In the language of the elitist economist, margin means change; utility means satisfaction. Marginal utility therefore means additional satisfaction derived from some change--generally additional consumer goods or additional income. The economic law of diminishing marginal utility states that *less additional utility is derived from each additional unit of consumption*. This law is what makes the concept of marginal utility important.

An example used in an economics class by an elitist professor might provide clarification of the concept of marginal utility. A member of the class of economically disadvantaged humyns has been laboring intensively (perhaps caring for the lawns of economic oppressors) all day earning hi'r meager wages. Not having been allowed a break for lunch, the worker is almost totally consumed by hunger, thirst and exhaustion by the end of the workday. H'orsh' decides to spend a portion of the income of the day, little it may be, for a large pizza and large pitcher of hi'r favorite beverage at the local pizzeria. In exchange for the meal, the economically oppressed humyn will increase the wealth of the oppressive pizzeria owner by twenty dollars, plus a regressive tax payment to the local and state governments. Regressivity in taxes, which penalizes the economically oppressed, will be explained in the chapters on government and taxation.

After the oppressed humyn finishes the first large pizza and pitcher, the waitron asks her'm'it if h'orsh' would like another order of the same. The economically deprived humyn answers that while h'orsh' is not yet glutted, hi'r meager wages of the day will not support another order.

"But," says the waitron, "We have a special of the day. If you consume one order at full price, you may buy the same thing again for one dollar."

The law of demand, discussed previously, now takes over. While the oppressed humyn was willing, but not able to pay twenty dollars for a second pizza and pitcher, h'orsh' is quite willing and able to pay one dollar.

The second pizza and pitcher is consumed, but the oppressed worker does not derive nearly the satisfaction from the second order. Why? The hunger and thirst of the humyn has been partially sated.

Again the waitron approaches the patron.

"Did you enjoy your pizza and pitcher?"

"Yes," replies the economically oppressed consumer, "but not nearly so much as the first."

It should be pointed out that the waitron knows that h'orsh' did not enjoy the second pizza and pitcher as much as the first, but does not know why. Being economically deprived, the waitron was never allowed by oppressive Republicans to attend a college economics class.

"Would you like another?" asks the waitron.

"Certainly not," replies the patron, being able, but not willing, to buy another round for a dollar.

"We have an even better special," says the waitron. "Buy the first for twenty dollars, the second for one dollar, and you can buy the third for five cents."

"Oh, well," says the patron. "For five cents, I might as well."

This is an important aspect of the law of diminishing marginal utility. The oppressed worker was willing and able to spend twenty dollars of hi'r meager earnings for the first large pizza and pitcher because h'orsh' expected to receive twenty dollars worth of satisfaction through the act of consumption. H'orsh' did not expect to receive twenty dollars worth of satisfaction from the second unit and was therefore unwilling to pay that amount. H'orsh' did expect to receive one dollar's worth of satisfaction, however.

Not even one dollar in additional satisfaction was expected from the third unit. But the patron was willing and able to pay only five cents, figuring at least that much satisfaction would be derived.

Quite the reverse was true. After consuming the third large pizza and pitcher, the oppressed patron regurgitated on the table the entirety of the three pizzas and three pitchers that h'orsh' had consumed that evening and was banished from the pizzeria for life. The following illustrates the marginal utility of pizza consumption.

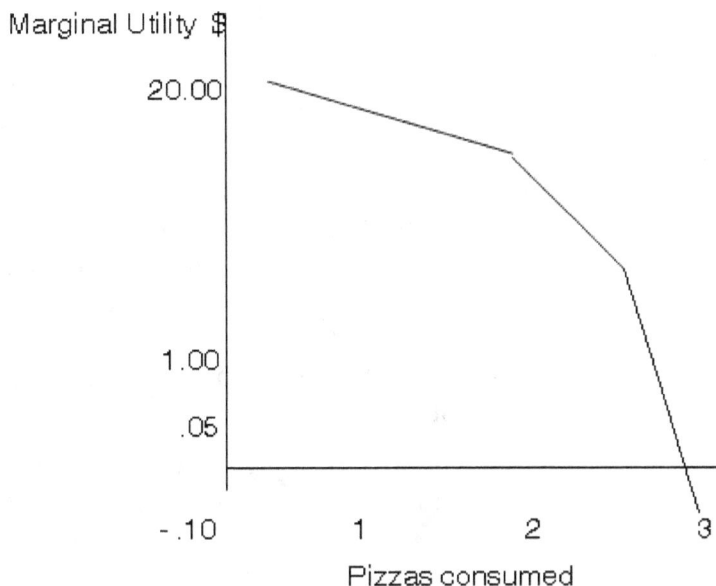

Marginal Utility $

```
20.00 ┤
       │
       │
       │
 1.00 ┤
  .05 ┤
       └─────────┬─────────┬─────────┬──
 -.10        1         2         3
                Pizzas consumed
```

By the time our tired, hungry oppressed worker consumes the third pizza, hi'r marginal utility is negative, requiring payment to consume another pizza.

It is also interesting to note that, as was discussed previously, the law of diminishing marginal utility is one of the major reasons that the law of demand holds true. Since all species of animality get less additional satisfaction from each additional unit of consumption, h'orsh' is willing and able to pay less for that additional unit. A lion with a sated appetite will not risk battle with another lion for the carcass of a terminally inconvenienced gazelle. A lion on the verge of starvation will nearly always risk its own viability and battle another, perhaps larger, lion for the same carcass.

The law of diminishing marginal utility has provided answers to questions that had long puzzled economists prior to the law's derivation. For example: Why would a humyn pay five thousand dollars to buy a frivolously luxurious one-carat diamond ring, and later that same day refuse to pay twenty-five cents for a glass of water at a restaurant? H'orsh' would still refuse to pay, even after the waitron explains that because of an extreme water shortage, the restaurant is being forced to make the charge. Such behavior seems logically inconsistent.

The law of diminishing marginal utility provides the answer. This is probably the economically advantaged humyn's first one-carat diamond ring and h'orsh' expects to get five thousand dollars in satisfaction from that unit of consumption. The glass of water could have been her ninth or tenth of the day. H'orsh' does not expect to get even twenty-five cents in satisfaction from the expenditure. Hence h'orsh'it refuses to buy the water, even though water is life sustaining and of much more value than the frivolous diamond ring.

It should also be emphasized that the purchase of a diamond ring is not a politically correct move in the first place. Diamond production is almost entirely controlled by DeBeers, a company of South Africa that is a major center of oppression against members of the African Diaspora and other sun-

persons who comprise the majority of the world population.

Now consider a set of entirely different circumstances. Imagine that the economically privileged humyn is now stranded in a desert and is in the process of perishing due to thirst. The oppressor has been crawling across the sand for days when h'orsh' sees a concession stand with a sign that reads, "Ice Cold Water--25 Cents". The perishing humyn crawls to the stand and asks the owner and economic exploiter for a free drink, explaining that h'orsh' left hi'r purse on the desert floor two days ago since it was too heavy to carry. The economic exploiter replies, "The drink will cost twenty-five cents. There will be no free water."

The formerly economically privileged, now economically exploited, humyn hastily makes a decision. "I have only this diamond ring for which I recently paid five thousand dollars. Will you take it in exchange for a drink of water?"

Again, the law of diminishing marginal utility is in action. The amount of satisfaction to be received from that first drink of water in days is easily worth the five thousand dollar diamond ring.

The law of diminishing marginal utility provides an obvious justification for complete equality of income. If income were equal among all, the last dollar earned would mean the same to all and the economy would operate at a higher level of efficiency. The greater the variation in marginal utility, the less efficiency there is in the economy. There exists an inverse relationship between income and marginal utility. The economically deprived, working for subsistence wages, receive much greater satisfaction from a few dollars than do economically advantaged oppressors, earning hundreds of thousands of dollars annually.

One additional dollar in income provides a disadvantaged humyn more satisfaction than it does an oppressive capitalist. Poor children will scramble, even fight, for a dollar found lying on the sidewalk. A white male oppressor making hundreds of thousands dollars a year might not go to the trouble to pick it up because one additional dollar in income does not mean very much. It will certainly not be worth the bending effort.

The last dollar earned does not mean very much to the economically advantaged and they will be quite willing to rid themselves of lesser valued dollars by purchasing frivolous luxuries, satisfying chemical preferences and the like. The necessities of life are taken for granted and since each additional dollar earned has little value to the oppressive rich, prices for necessities are driven up. Because of higher prices, necessities of life are often not available for the economically and motivationally deficient. Frivolous luxuries are overproduced because additional dollars mean very little to the economically advantaged. Necessities are underproduced because capitalist oppressors can make more profit by producing frivolous luxuries. The following illustrates the marginal utility of the last dollar earned.

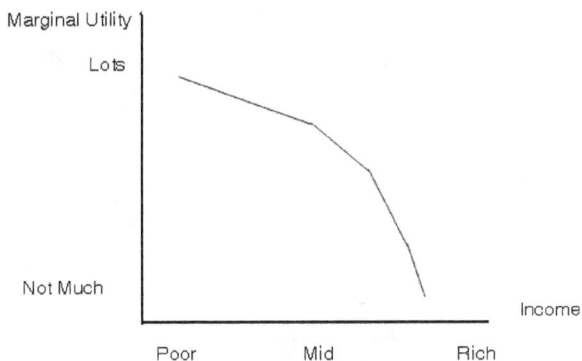

To the economically marginalized and motivationally deficient, frivolous luxuries are not even a consideration. There can be no chemical preference. Whatever is available on the street at a cheap price is bought regardless of risk.

With differing degrees of marginal utility, the economy must produce different products. It must produce expensive, frivolous luxuries for the rich, to whom money means little, and basic necessities for the poor, to whom money means a lot. Production of frivolous luxuries is considered a wasteful use of our scarce economic resources. If all humyns were equal, that is, each received the same amount of income, each individual would receive the same amount of satisfaction from the last dollar earned. This would result in economic efficiency because only goods that everyone would want would be produced. There would be no Cadillacs, Lincoln Continentals, Hummers and sport utility vehicles that are produced for only the privileged few. If all humyns had the same income, the economy would produce a car that provides each driver the same amount of satisfaction. To ensure quality and style that would be pleasing to all, Congress would appoint a select committee to oversee the design and production of this ultimate car.

Economic efficiency does have its detractors. Italian economist Vilfredo Pareto hypothesized that as long as economic resources were not being used efficiently, one humyn could be made better off without making another worse off. Once a state of economic efficiency is reached, if one humyn makes a gain of some sort, then another must suffer an equal loss. It need not be said that this "zero sum" situation does not sit well with capitalist oppressors. They would all prefer to increase their riches together. The economically oppressed do not care.

If all incomes were equal at the mid level, all would value the last dollar earned equally. Marginal utility would be very high and the same for each individual, regardless of status in life. The economy would therefore produce goods and services that would be desired equally by all. No wasteful frivolous luxuries would be produced.

The economy will have, through the establishment of equal marginal utility, reached a state of absolute efficiency.

CH.7: THE GROSS DOMESTIC PRODUCT

Gross domestic product, hereafter referred to as simply GDP, is a measure of economic performance. It attempts to measure, in dollars, the final market value of the total amount of production occurring over one year within the borders of the United States. The government determines the amount produced by measuring the amount spent on the purchase of goods and services by the four major spending groups-- consumers, businesses, governments and foreigners. The assumption is that what has been produced must be bought or placed in inventory by business. The GDP has been likened by one elitist economist to a gigantic checkout counter over which every item manufactured in the United States passes. At the end of the year, the grand total at the bottom of the miles-long cash register tape would be the GDP. This is essentially true in simple-minded terms. However, problems abound because economists who developed the concept of GDP in the first place and those who collect and analyze current data have never been members of the oppressed category of humyns.

Consumer spending, symbolized by the letter C, is the amount spent by humyns as they consume the various goods and services produced by oppressive businesses.

Government spending, symbolized by the letter G, represents the total purchases of goods and services by Federal, state and local governments. This includes all government sponsored construction of post offices, military bases and housing, court houses, highways, bridges, water and sewage systems and any other government projects one can think of. This has the unusual effect that government does not invest. Once a $10 million post office is built in a rural community, it immediately has no value. Many have said that if the government used generally accepted accounting procedures and government infrastructure were considered an asset to be depreciated over the years, the Federal budget could be balanced in a very short time. Government spending is counted only if the government receives something for its money. Salaries of government employees and transfers to the economically oppressed and motivationally deficient are not included.

Spending by business, properly called gross private domestic investment, is symbolized by the letter I. Gross means that all investment, both new investment and replacement investment, is counted. Private investment means that only investment by private business in counted. Investment by governments, such as spending for new highways and post offices, is not included. Domestic investment is investment within the borders of the United States regardless of the nationality of the business. The building of factories in foreign countries by American companies does not count. Changes in business inventories are included in calculation of investment to correct for goods that have been produced during the current year but not yet sold, and also those goods that are sold during the current year but produced during the previous year.

The final dimension of GDP is net exports, symbolized by (X - M), where X is exports and M is imports. The purpose of net exports is to add those goods that were produced in the United States and shipped to foreign countries, and therefore never crossed the great check-out counter, and to subtract those goods produced by foreign countries but counted as GDP under C, G or I. Net exports is traditionally a negative number, meaning that we have for years imported more goods than we have exported.

The GDP is the total of C + G + I + (X - M)

The following table shows the amount of GDP for each component for 2008 in billions of dollars:

GDP Component	Amount	% of total
Consumer	10,190.7	70.6
Government	2,945.8	20.4
Investment	1,999.4	13.9
Net Exports	-706.1	-4.9
	14,429.2	100

An interesting note is that GDP first exceeded one trillion dollars in 1970. I was in graduate school in 1975 and my finance professor was still in a state of disbelief. The GDP has increased at a still more unbelievable rate since.

Politically incorrect problems of the GDP, as a measure of total production, abound. Two serious defects of the GDP are the twin problems of composition and distribution. The GDP does not determine the particular combination of goods and services produced, only the total dollar amount of their final market value. Nor does it consider for whom the goods are produced. The economy could be producing massive amounts of frivolous luxuries for the privileged class and still appear to be performing magnificently, which is indeed the case. The economically marginalized cannot afford such luxuries as large SUVs, yachts and private airplanes that add large individual amounts to the GDP. The contribution to total production made by this oppressed group of humyns, measured as the amount they spend, is therefore insignificant. Goods that would increase happiness of the entire population are underproduced in favor of frivolous luxuries for the privileged few.

The GDP does not measure the quality of goods produced. The erroneous assumption is sometimes made that there exists a relationship between quality and cost but that correlation has not been shown. Compare the quality of Japanese cars with some of their more expensive American-made counterparts.

Another major problem results because of the underground economy. A product or service that does not go through the capitalist market is never considered as "produced" and does not contribute to the GDP. Since a disproportionate number of economically exploited humyns do not work within the established capitalistic market, their contributions to the economy are not officially recognized. For example, the economically marginalized may care for capitalist oppressors' lawns and gardens, cutting grass and trimming hedges for their meager wages. They accept only cash to avoid the embarrassment of attempting to redeem spendable money for their small paychecks. Since these expenditures by privileged landowners are never recorded by the capitalist banking system, the disadvantaged lawn-maintenance humyn does not receive credit for hi'r contribution to the GDP.

The contribution to domestic output made by those who are engaged in illegal activities is not counted because those transactions also do not go through the capitalist market. Many of the oppressed are forced to sell drugs for small profits in order to obtain the necessities of life. The differently motivated who are not permanently employed and are forced to break oppressive and unwise laws receive no credit at all for their contributions to production.

It should by now be patently obvious that the gross domestic product is a device created by oppressive economically advantaged humyns to measure how well they themselves are doing, not the economy as a whole. Major revisions must be made, primarily in the areas of composition and distribution, if the GDP is to provide appropriate data in a politically correct economy. Production of frivolous luxuries, which benefit only the economically privileged, must be severely constrained if not completely eliminated. Federal, state and local governments must ensure that goods and services are equally distributed among all, regardless of economic status.

Steps must be taken to ensure that contributions of the economically marginalized and differently motivated are included in production data. One reason these deprived classes avoid the capitalist market is the existing tax structure. The economically exploited should be excused from all tax payments while privileged classes should be taxed of all excess income. Excess income is that income above the amount required to purchase the necessities of life. If a state of equality existed among all citizens, then the economic contributions of all citizens would be treated equally.

Finally, the current prison population shows that a disproportionate number of the economically exploited are forced into selling drugs in order to survive. It is also true that the illegal drug industry is one of the largest industries in the country, generating well over a trillion dollars. The sale of all drugs should be immediately legalized to provide credit to the economically marginalized and differently motivated for their contributions to the economy, reduce the number of oppressed humyns in prison and to increase the GDP.

CH.8: THE PRIVATE SECTOR

Any economy is composed of two sectors: the private sector, which includes households and businesses; and the public sector, which includes all governments--local, state and Federal. The politically incorrect private sector is concerned with personal utility and profit, serving only the ambitious and self-centered. It is for this reason that the private sector has been solely responsible for increasing inequality among all American humyns. Nonhumyn animals have no rights at all! The more politically correct public sector is concerned with social welfare, serving the best interests of the economically marginalized and differently motivated. The primary role of the Federal government, as the major economic unit of the public sector, must be to ensure equality of all species of animality.

HOUSEHOLDS

The major component of the private sector, the household, is an economic unit composed of one or more humyns and their nonhumyn companions. All humyns, other than the oppressed homeless, are members of some household. The oppressed can be members of households, as long as they are not homeless. The household is therefore a family unit, no matter how big, which plays two important roles in the economy. The first is that of resource supplier. Households own all resources--labor, land and capital. If an oppressive business owner wants to purchase a resource of any type to be used in the production of a good or service, h'orsh' must purchase that resource from some exploited household.

The second important role of the household is that of consumer. Householders use the meager payments received from supplying resources to oppressive business owners to purchase products manufactured using resources that consumers themselves supply. It is therefore necessary to examine householders as income receivers, or resource suppliers, and spenders.

In a capitalist economy, householders receive income through the sale of economic resources to business. Since some householders are business-owning entrepreneurs, householders as a group may also be divided into oppressors and the oppressed. Wages, generated by the sale of labor, constitute about seventy-five percent of the income of householders. This group of householders who must work for others in order to receive their meager wages comprises the oppressed. The other twenty-five percent of income, interest from leasing capital equipment and rent from land, goes to oppressive profit-seeking capitalist entrepreneurs and advantaged landowners.

The capitalist system of compensation for resources leads to inequality. Humyn resources that oppressive business owners consider the most valuable, the college educated and the overly motivated, receive the most pay. The cerebrally challenged and motivationally dispossessed must be satisfied with subsistence wages. The top five percent of the income earners receive about twenty percent of total income in the United States; the poorest twenty percent receive less than five percent. The top twenty percent receive about fifty percent of total income. The following table shows the distribution of income by quintiles in 2005:

Quintile	Share (%)
Top20%	50.4
Next 20%	23.0
Next 20%	14.6
Next 20%	8.6
Bottom 20%	3.4

When wealth is considered, inequality among humyns under United States capitalism is even worse. Wealth consists of all assets of a household minus the total liabilities of the household. Assets include savings, stocks and bonds, automobiles, business ownership and real property. Liabilities include money owed on mortgages, consumer debt, automobile loans, and any other household debt. The wealthiest one percent of humyns in the United States own over thirty percent of all wealth. The top ten percent owns about seventy percent of all wealth. This means that the bottom ninety percent owns about thirty percent. What is even worse, the wealthiest one-half of one percent owns over twenty-five percent of all the wealth in this country, almost as much as the bottom ninety percent! The following table shows the distribution of wealth ownership in 2001:

% of Owners	Share %
Top 0.5	25.6
Next 0.5	8.4
Next 4	23.4
Next 5	11.4
Next 10	12.8
Bottom 80	18.4

The data in the above table are in agreement with the 80/20 rule, created by Italian economist Vilfredo Pareto in 1906. He observed that twenty percent of humyns owned eighty percent of total wealth and that the other eighty percent of humyns owned the remaining twenty percent. The wealth distribution is worse today because many of the poor lost their homes during the depression of 2008. The depression was the result of greedy capitalists convincing the poor to buy mansions they couldn't afford.

It is no wonder that there is little or no upward mobility within the capitalist economy. Once a person becomes a member of the economically marginalized class, it is likely that h'orsh' shall continue to be exploited for life. The one-half of one percent of the population who are the true capitalist oppressors keep the economically marginalized in their places!

Householders constitute the major spending group in the economy. About seventy percent of the gross domestic product is supported by personal consumption expenditures. Householders spend about fifteen percent of their income for durable goods, which include automobiles, computers, videocassette recorders, washing machines and the like. Many of these goods are luxuries and are not within the budgets of the economically oppressed. About thirty percent of income is spent on nondurable goods that include food, clothes, gasoline, fuel and other necessities of life. About half of householders' income is spent on services such as housing, medical care, transportation, haircuts, lawn service and the like.

Nondurable goods are goods that are expected to last less than three years; durables are expected to last longer than three years. Sometimes the difference between the two gets a little fuzzy. As a personal example, I once had a pair of blue jeans that outlasted three Fords. My wife first threw them away when they were about fifteen years old because they had a hole in the seat. I rescued them while taking the trash out and brought them back in. My wife asked what should we do with them. I said we could patch them. "What color?" she said. I said, "Red." So she put a red iron-on patch in the seat. A few years later, she threw them out again because they had holes in both knees. I again rescued them and now had red patches on both knees. When I wore them to the shopping mall, teenagers would look at them and marvel. She threw them out again when the knee patches wore out. I again rescued them and she said, "What now?" I said, "Cut them off." So I had cut-offs. The last time I saw those jeans was when my granddaughter was wearing them as part of a clown costume with rope suspenders on Halloween night. Those jeans saw more than twenty years of use.

And the government says blue jeans are nondurable goods while Ford (and Chevrolet and Chrysler) cars are durables.

Politically incorrect economists say that the amount spent for services is indicative of our economy being one of service rather than manufacturing. This conclusion does not reflect an entirely accurate analysis of the data. The fifty percent spent for services is more likely reflective of conspicuous consumption by the economically advantaged as they try to keep up with and even outdo their neighbors. You will again recall that the richest twenty percent receive more than fifty percent of total income--the amount spent on services. Few of the economically marginalized can afford lawn services, artificial fingernails, pedicures or new hairdos with color. They spend their meager incomes on necessary nondurables and interest payments to finance the durable goods for which they have an absolute need.

The portion of disposable income not spent for consumption of goods and services is defined as savings. Compared with the rest of the world,

American households do not save very much of their earnings, less then four percent. German and Japanese households save between fifteen and twenty percent of their incomes. Further, nearly all saving in American households is done by the economically privileged. Economically deprived wage earners generally live payday to payday, from public assistance rightful share of one month to public assistance rightful share of the next month. Franco Modigliani was actually awarded a Nobel prize in economics in 1985 for discovering that most saving is done by those who are willing and able to save. Who among even the most gray-matter challenged did not already know that? Since Nobel prizes are worth a million dollars or more, this is obviously a case of white Eurocentric male oppressors taking care of other white Eurocentric male oppressors. A Nobel Prize in economics has never been awarded to a member of the African Diaspora or a vaginal humyn of alternative cultural or sexual orientation.

Generally speaking, if we want to save more, then the amount we spend for consumption must decrease. Our standard of living will become progressively lower. If we decide to conspicuously consume a few frivolous luxuries in order to gain more satisfaction from life, then our savings must decrease. Consumption and saving schedules move in opposite directions.

Consuming and saving are not the only things we do with our personal income. We also must pay taxes. Disposable income is personal income minus personal taxes. Changes in taxes cause both consumption and savings to move in the same direction. If governments take in taxes more of our personal income, disposable income decreases and we have less to spend and save. If governments take in taxes less of our personal income, disposable income increases and we have more to spend or save, as we like. Taxes are such an important subject that our in-depth discussion of them will be deferred until a later chapter. However, a few general remarks are appropriate at this time.

The individual personal income tax, which brings in about forty-five percent of total revenue, is the major revenue source for the Federal government. Close behind are Social Security, Medicare, unemployment, retirement and other payroll taxes, which bring in about thirty-seven percent. It is important to note that primarily oppressed workers pay these taxes, comprising about eighty percent of total Federal revenue. Taxes paid by the economically advantaged comprise the other twenty percent. These include corporate income taxes, excise taxes, estate and gift taxes, customs duties and other business taxes.

States derive most of their revenue from the general sales tax while local governments depend heavily on the property tax. Both of these taxes are regressive in that they force the economically deprived to pay taxes at a higher rate than the economically privileged. A more complete discussion of taxes and their implications for a politically correct economy will be found in a later chapter.

BUSINESSES

It is sometimes difficult to separate businesses from households because householders own all the businesses. While most householders work for wages, those who own and operate businesses obtain what is known as proprietor's income. They receive a combination of wages for their labor, rent for the land they own, interest for their capital equipment and loans to the economically oppressed, and entrepreneur's profit because they bear the risk of production. Successful proprietors are in the twenty percent of higher income householders who receive fifty percent of total income and are capitalist oppressors. The other eighty percent of householders comprise the economically deprived.

Businesses can be either large or small. Small businesses are usually one-plant firms in which financially challenged sole proprietors do virtually all the work. They sometimes have a few employees over whom they can exercise oppressive power. It cannot be said that small-business humyns are oppressors, however, because they too are oppressed. The one characteristic shared by all small business owners is that they want their businesses to become big so that they, too, can become true oppressors.

Before their businesses can grow, struggling owners must receive approval from owners of the American banking system. This approval is granted in the form of loans to finance capital growth and is the major source of oppression to small business owners. Economic exploiters will supply the needed loan only if they believe the financially challenged business can be successful enough to repay the principal amount of the loan plus usurious interest charges. However, if the future of the small business looks overly bright, the financial exploiters will not lend the business humyn money, but will seize the growing business for themselves. The former owner who was struggling to become a major oppressor will now become one of the oppressed and be forced to work for a subsistence wage. It is as Karl Marx, the most politically correct social economist, predicted.

Capitalism as an economic system is subject to up and down cycles — periods of boom and bust, inflation and recession. The following graph depicts a theoretical business cycle, measured over time by Gross Domestic Product. Notice periods of recession, depression, recovery, boom and peak

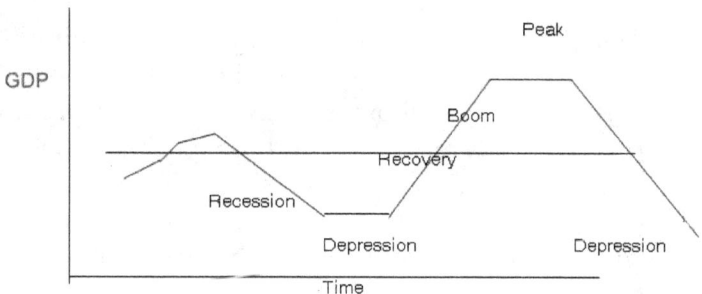

GDP

Peak

Boom

Recovery

Recession

Depression

Depression

Time

Business cycles can be caused by decreases or increases in spending by consumers or businesses, lending practices of oppressive bankers, technological progress, and external shocks such as wars, oil prices, and world conflicts that cause uncertainty in national markets. Whatever the cause, ups and downs of the business cycle affect different people in different ways.

110

According to Marx in *Das Kapital*, the capitalist economy consists of two types of people: oppressed proletariats (wage earners) and capitalists (oppressive business owners). Each is affected differently by ups and downs of the economy. With each cycle of recession, weaker businesses will fail and be taken over by larger, more financially secure businesses. The already large businesses will become even larger. Formerly oppressive owners of failed businesses will now become members of the oppressed class. As inflationary cycles occur, oppressive business owners will raise prices to further exploit the economically marginalized. Fewer and fewer businesses will exist and the number of humyns who are among the economically oppressed will grow larger and larger. Eventually, the business community will consist of a very few large monopolies owned by nonvaginal white oppressive humyns. The number of oppressed proletariats will increase drastically. As more and more former capitalists become members of the proletariat, less and less of the population will be financially able to purchase goods manufactured by the decreasing number of capitalists. There will not be enough customers to further enrich the remaining capitalists. They will be forced to reduce wages to increase profits. Wages will be reduced until all proletariats are on subsistence, poverty wages. Working people will then arise, overthrow the existing order and establish a dictatorship of the proletariat. The state will wither away and a glorious state of pure communism will evolve.

The time may be right for the kind of revolution predicted by Marx. This will not be a revolution for communism, but a revolution to establish a politically correct business environment. Laws will be passed to limit the influence of white, Eurocentric, nonvaginal humyns on current society.

Vaginal humyns, which comprise fifty-one percent of our current population, have for years been referred to by government agencies as "housewives." In a politically correct society, wofems will, because of their majority status, be recognized as legal heads of households. Some states currently require that license plates for motor vehicles owned by a household be renewed on the birthday of the nonvaginal partner. Such practices are sexist and, after the politically correct revolution, will be illegal.

At least fifty-one percent of businesses will be owned by wimyn. Businesses will be seized from nonvaginal humyns in order to attain this goal.

Representation in Congress will by law be fifty-one percent vaginal.

It will be illegal for the salaries of nonvaginal humyns to exceed those of vaginal humyns.

Vaginal humyns, primarily those of color, will dominate the Federal Reserve Board of Governors and control the American banking system. The American banking system will preserve the politically correct business environment by ceasing to lend money to oppressive capitalists and lend money only to the economically deprived who really need it.

CH.9: THE PUBLIC SECTOR

The public sector consists of all components of Federal, state and local governments that have the moral responsibility to establish and maintain economic and social equality among all humyns. According to standard economics textbooks, the role of government varies according to the type of economy. In all economies, government and the market structure share the responsibility for making economic decisions. In a capitalistic economy, the market makes all major economic decisions and governments play only a minor role. In a politically correct economy, governments are the primary decision-making bodies, with the Federal government taking the lead.

Politically incorrect economists think the market system is more efficient than a government-driven economy because the market, with its producers driven by the profit motive, will produce those things that humyns want to buy at a price they can afford to pay. Otherwise, greedy capitalists will not be able to make their obscene profits. This is the basis of Adam Smith's "invisible hand" analogy, in which he states that producers are guided by the market, as by an "invisible hand," to do those things that benefit society, even though that was not their original intent. Their original intent is, of course, to make profit. He was naive in thinking that giving consumers what they want at prices they can afford is beneficial. Consumers are not prepared to make decisions about how to best spend their meager incomes and must receive guidance from an informative government. Uninformed members of society would otherwise spend their money on frivolous luxuries and habit-forming drugs.

In a politically correct economy, government assumes an increasingly important role. The politically enlightened realize that the government knows better what is good for the people than the people themselves do. In a perfect economy, the government would provide goods all humyns need at a price they can afford because everything would be free!

Even under capitalism, the government must play some role in the economy. In the United States, Federal, state and local governments sponsor about twenty percent of total production. Even though the participation of government in the economy has increased from less than ten percent since the Great Depression, this proportion must increase even more if a politically correct economy is to succeed.

One important role of government is of course to provide a medium of exchange. This could be a monetary system, as is used in nearly all countries of the world, or a more politically correct voucher system for specific goods, which would discourage the conspicuous consumption of frivolous luxuries by the economically advantaged. Some form of money, whether specie or vouchers, is necessary to overcome the problems associated with a barter system.

Another important function of government is regulation of business. As long as the capitalist market exists, government must ensure that the price system remains competitive. As Karl Marx predicted, an uncontrolled capitalist economy will through evolution become a monopolistic economy controlled by a very few oppressive business conglomerates. It will then be easy for one large producer to withhold any product, create an artificial shortage and thereby cause an increase in price. It is the responsibility of the Federal government to strictly enforce antitrust laws to ensure that monopolies do not form.

In a politically correct economy, monopolies would not be a problem. Government would make all production decisions and exercise complete price control, making all goods affordable to all. The market would cease to be a factor.

The market is inherently inefficient in making production decisions. In their selfish quest for profit, producers manufacture large quantities of frivolous and obscene luxuries for the privileged few. The government must correct for this misallocation of precious resources.

Another reason for government interference in capitalist markets is that oppressive producers will, to further increase their already excessive profits, attempt to pass parts of their production costs off to society as a whole. These "external" costs are generally in the form of environmental damage. It is less expensive for a pulp and paper mill to discharge its pollutants into a river, killing all forms of aquatic life, both animal and nonanimal, than it is to implement an expensive process to clean up the pollutants itself. An excellent example of this type of external cost is the Fenholloway River in rural Taylor County, Florida. The river was once fed by a spring of pure sulfur water, which was bottled and sold, as a cure for arthritis and other health problems, to the economically oppressed who could not afford other expensive medical treatment. The river was a fisher's and sports humyn's haven, with plentiful bass, bream and hunting along the river's banks. The mouth of the river was home to several fish camps, providing easy access to the grass beds of the Gulf of Mexico with an abundance of speckled trout and red drum waiting to provide food for the tables of the poor and oppressed. Disaster came in 1947 when Buckeye Cellulose, Inc., then a division of the Proctor and Gamble Corporation, wanted to build a pulp mill aside the river and dump its waste into the river for a slow twenty-mile journey to the Gulf. Local politicians saw jobs and money. Nobody thought about damage to the environment.

In April of 1947, both the foolish Florida House of representatives and the Florida Senate voted unanimously to declare the Fenholloway an "industrial" river. Those who live along the river no longer drink sulfur water for their health, but are advised to see their doctor, and perhaps their lawyer, if they become ill. Fish in the river have begun to exhibit strange characteristics. Red drum and speckled trout, once abundant in the grass beds in the mouth of the river, have gone elsewhere or died. Those who owned fish camps or sulfur water bottling plants had to find other occupations.

116

It is obvious that the more production costs that can be passed to society as a whole, the less of the costs will be paid by the producer and the greater the profit for the exploiters of the environment. As production costs decrease and per-unit profits increase, the more the offending business will produce. Business will therefore tend to overallocate valuable resources owned by all members of society to lines of production in which external costs are involved.

Government must correct for this misallocation of resources by reinternalizing external costs--that is, increase the costs of production of the offending business by at least an amount equal to the cost being passed to society.

There are several ways that governments can force reinternalization of external costs. One method is regulation or legislation. Governments can simply declare such action illegal and use the power of the law to make the offending company stop polluting. Governments may also sell pollution rights to businesses, ensuring that pollution is kept within tolerable limits. Lawsuits may be filed. Either government or private citizens can sue businesses to force cleanups of polluted areas. The problem with these methods is that the responsibility for corrections of resource misallocation is placed on the offending business of the private sector. Cheating is rampant as "books are cooked" to show that cleanup has occurred. All know that government is better prepared than the market to allocate society's scarce resources. The method preferred by the politically correct is to levy against offending businesses a pollution tax in at least the amount of all external costs.

Government can then use the revenue derived from this tax to clean up the environmental damage or for any other purpose the politically correct may consider more important.

Another important advantage of a pollution tax is that the tax need not be limited to the amount of external costs. The government can punish, even bankrupt, business by taxing excessive amounts. Undesirable businesses--such as those in the tobacco, alcoholic spirits, oil, and fast food industries--can therefore be completely eliminated. This is also true of any other business tax. Taxes constitute the most powerful weapon available to a politically correct government.

A problem of a different type exists if the offending company is a politically correct enterprise owned by struggling oppressed humyns. In this case it is recommended that governments reward the businesses by cash payments or tax credits if the owners promise to cease all practices that may result in environmental damage.

Government must reallocate resources for production of public goods--goods that are owned by society as a whole and are open to everybody. Libraries, museums, schools, parks, public television stations, highway systems and statues of distinguished politicians are examples. Since no one can be excluded from using a public good (economists call this the free-rider problem), a profit cannot be made and the public good will not be provided through the capitalist market. The provision of the good or service is therefore the responsibility of government. The amount and type of public goods to be supplied, however, is a source of contention among members of legislative bodies. The result is that public goods are generally distributed based on politics, a practice the politically correct see as unacceptable. The most powerful members of Congress get the bulk of public goods for their districts, thereby purchasing the votes of their constituents to ensure reelection.

Even the most politically incorrect economists believe that some public goods are necessary. Their acid test is whether the good could be provided through the market. For example, if a road is needed between Acidville and Baseville, then someone should be able to build it and make a profit by charging tolls. If a profit cannot be made, then it is doubtful that a road is actually needed. Conversely, politically correct economists believe that if anyone else in the country has a road, the citizens of Acidville and Baseville deserve one of equal quality, regardless of traffic load or need. All goods currently provided through the market should be assessed to determine their suitability as public goods. It will be discovered that nearly all consumer goods including food, clothing, shelter and transportation, other than frivolous luxuries, will fit into this category. These goods are to be produced by government for free distribution to all.

The fourth economic responsibility of government, which many consider its most important, is to bring stability to the economy--to eliminate periods of recession and inflation. Theory holds that if the economy is in recession, it is because total demand is too low. Business will not produce goods that cannot be sold. They will cut back on production and lay employees off. The government must stimulate the economy by increasing total demand. Taxes can be decreased so that householders can buy more goods and services. Another way is for the government itself to increase its spending. If the economy is experiencing inflation, it is because total demand is too high--more goods are being demanded than can be produced. Government must bring inflation down by decreasing aggregate demand. Taxes should be increased on the rich to take spending power away from economic oppressors who spend excessive amounts of money on frivolous luxuries. The government itself can decrease spending to decrease total demand, but this is not recommended because the already oppressed would suffer through loss of government benefits.

The politically correct way for government to control the economy is to increase government spending during recessions and to increase taxes during inflation. It would be destructive to the politically correct movement for responsible, motivated economically advantaged workers to experience actual tax cuts. They could quickly become accustomed to them and expect even more tax cuts in the future.

Because many elite economists consider stabilization as the most important economic function of the Federal government, stabilization will be discussed more deeply in the following chapter.

This said, the politically correct believe that stabilization is of secondary importance. The most important responsibility of government is to redistribute income. The supreme goal of economic reform is for all humyns to be equal. The government should use its power to tax to achieve this goal, transferring money from the advantaged class to the economically marginalized and differently motivated.

Finally, the government should develop legislation and regulation to accomplish the preceding functions. Rules by which business can operate must be specified. Government must pass laws to punish offending businesses, to end cycles of recession and inflation, to provide public goods and to ensure equality of all.

CH.10: THE ECONOMIC FUNCTIONS OF GOVERNMENT: STABILIZATION

According to politically correct Keynesian economic theory, the primary determinant of economic stability is total demand for goods and services. You will recall from the previous chapter that if total demand is too low, businesses will stop producing products that are not bought. Workers will be laid off and the economy will go into recession. The newly unemployed will be unable to purchase goods and services, thereby further lowering demand and even more workers will be laid off. They, too, will be unable to purchase new goods and still more workers are laid off. This multiplier effect, that loss of income for one results in the loss of income for another, will continue and the economy will go from recession into depression. Conversely, if total demand is too high there will be a shortage of goods and services. Businesses will not be able to produce everything that is demanded and prices will be bid up by greedy, economically privileged consumers. There will be the classic situation in which too many dollars are chasing too few goods and the economy will enter inflation. Both recession and inflation are destructive to the economically marginalized and differently motivated.

The multiplier is such an important concept in Keynesian economics that it is perhaps deserving of further explanation and can be best understood by a simple example. Suppose Charlie gets a ten-dollar wage increase. He will say, as most of us do, "I'm going to save every bit of it." That will never happen. He will more than likely save about two dollars and spend eight of his newly found riches. Charlie decides to buy a fishing rod from his pal Joe. Charlie's ten-dollar pay raise, along with Joe's eight dollars for the fishing rod, has now generated a total of eighteen dollars in income.

Following economic tradition, Joe will also try to save the entire eight dollars for his future but will be unsuccessful. He will spend about eighty percent, or $6.40 of his new income. He decides to buy a golf glove from his friend Harry. Charlie's pay raise has now generated a total of $24.40 in new income. Harry will now spend about eighty percent, or $5.12 of his new income to buy an exercise wheel for his hamster from his friend Mollie. Charlie's little raise has now generated $29.52 of new income. That's how the multiplier works. We spend a portion of any new income we get, providing new income for someone else. The multiplier also works in the opposite direction. Suppose Charlie had received a pay cut of ten dollars. He would have spent eight dollars less at the local Dixie store. The owner of the Dixie store would have spent $6.40 less to have his lawn mowed. The lawn mowing humyn would have had $5.12 less to spend at the tavern Friday night, and so it goes. How much total income will be increased or decreased from a given change in income for an individual? This depends on something elite economists call the *marginal propensity to consume (MPC),* which means the proportion of any change in income that goes to or takes away from consumption. The larger the MPC the greater the increase or decrease in income. In case you are interested, the formula used by economists is 1/(1 - MPC). The MPC used in our example is .8 and the multiplier is 1/.2, or five. Charlie's ten-dollar change in income will therefore result in a change in total income of fifty bucks. The multiplier also works on a national scale. Suppose the government cuts spending by a billion dollars, which is really not much in a total budget of over three trillion dollars. With our assumption of MPC = .8, the result would be a total decrease in income and spending of five billion.

Complicating attempts to calculate the multiplier is the fact that Americans are the poorest savers in the world. In 2004, Americans spent an average 98.2 percent of their current income. Americans have often spent more than they made, going deeply into debt. It is highly likely that Americans will spend a major portion or perhaps all of any increase in disposable income. Assume all of any increase in income is spent. The multiplier would be an impossible one divided by zero. Theoretically the economy would just grow and grow and grow. The problem for the United States economy is that consumers would likely spend their newly found riches at Wal-Mart, and the ten thousand or so factories in China that depend on Wal-Mart to distribute their products would just grow and grow and grow.

The following graph shows the trend of the multiplier as the MPC increases.

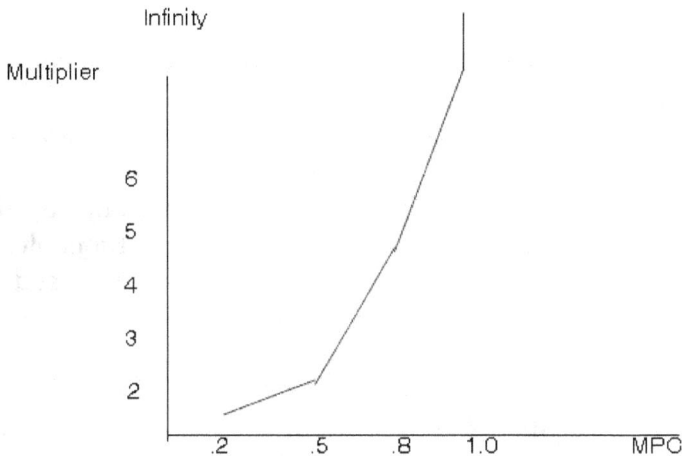

In the real world, the multiplier is not easily calculated because no one knows exactly what the MPC is. The only true way to determine the multiplier is after the fact. We can determine the change in total income, which is fairly easy. This figure is estimated quarterly when GDP data are gathered. Then we must wait for an extended period of time, perhaps years, for the multiplier to take effect. Cumulative GDP data can be examined to determine the change in total spending. We can then divide the change in consumer spending by the change in disposable income to determine the multiplier. The process is still a little iffy. If the change in total spending resulted from the change in disposable income and other factors have not intervened, we may have a pretty good estimate of the multiplier. But other factors do have an impact. As we have said before, economics is a rather inexact science.

When the economy enters recession, hourly workers receiving mere subsistence wages are the first to be laid off. This is especially true for unfortunate humyns working for oppressive big businesses that produce the capital goods and durable goods. These products including farm tractors, trucks, hand tools, automobiles and refrigerators that are expected to last several years. One characteristic common to capital and durable goods is that their purchases are postponable. In the case of capital goods, equipment used to produce other things, capitalist producers will not build a new factory or modernize an existing factory when they don't expect to be able to sell the things they will produce in that factory. Such action will be postponed until economic conditions improve. Economically oppressed workers who are engaged in the manufacture of capital goods will therefore be laid off until better economic times are expected. Likewise, economically marginalized workers will not commit themselves to a $600 monthly car payment for sixty months if they expect to be losing their jobs in the near future. The same holds for washing machines, refrigerators and furniture, which the oppressed must always buy on credit and then pay for through monthly payments. They will postpone the purchase of these items until economic times are better.

The second factor affecting oppressed employees of big business is monopoly power. If total demand is deficient, big businesses do not have to decrease prices, as small businesses often do, in order to sell their products. They instead decrease costs of production by laying off workers. If necessary, they will lay off all their workers, completely shut their businesses down and adjourn to their country clubs and play golf for the duration of the recession. The only ones to suffer are workers who are now denied even their meager subsistence wages. Indeed, during the Great Depression, production of capital and durable goods dropped by eighty percent while prices of these goods fell less than twenty percent. In comparison, production of agricultural commodities fell by only five percent while prices of such goods fell by more than sixty percent.

Inflation, an increase in the general level of prices, decreases the meager wages of oppressed workers even further. As prices increase, purchasing power decreases. This is devastating to those who are working for subsistence wages in the first place. It is true that inflation also causes wage increases, but price increases always precede wage increases by months, sometimes years. Workers already struggling to make ends meet therefore fall further and further behind.

A good way to determine the effects of inflation is to use the Rule of 70. Divide seventy by the annual inflation rate and we find the number of years necessary for prices to double. If the inflation rate is seven percent, prices will double in ten years. As a result, purchasing power of workers is cut in half. At a 1980s inflation rate of fourteen percent, prices would double in only five years. This is especially damaging to the lifestyles of the economically marginalized, including the elderly who must live on fixed incomes and the differently motivated or differently abled who depend upon public assistance for sustenance.

You will recall that the economically advantaged are not affected by inflation or recession but instead use economic cycles to further increase their riches. As a brief review, the rich lend money to the needy at usurious interest rates during periods of inflation. Financial holdings of advantaged oppressors also increase in value and may be sold at extremely high capital gain. During periods of recession, capitalists increase their financial holdings by taking over weak businesses at cheap prices. The businesses may then be sold at profits after another cycle of inflation. Periods of inflation and recession therefore further punish the oppressed and reward the oppressors. It is absolutely essential that government smooth economic cycles, eliminating recession and inflation, in order to prevent further inequality.

The primary tool for stabilizing the economy is fiscal policy, consisting of changes in government spending and taxation, advocated by John Maynard Keynes. It will be recalled that gross domestic product is the sum of spending by consumers, business, governments and foreign countries. This sum is also equal to total spending or total demand, represented by the formula $TS = C + I + G + X$. In order to bring the economy out of a recession caused by a deficiency of total spending, government must increase one or more of C, I, G or X. It is obvious that as total spending increases, gross domestic product also increases and the economy will enter a period of growth.

The method favored by the economically privileged, generally conservative politicians belonging to the Republican Party, is to cut taxes. The theory is that tax cuts leave money in the hands of householders who will in turn spend at least a major portion of it. Consumer spending ("C") will increase and the multiplier will kick in, causing a larger increase in total spending. That the rich favor tax cuts to stabilize the economy should come as no surprise. Tax cuts benefit only the rich because when tax cuts are used to stimulate the economy, all economic corrections are made through the market. The market system is a tool used by oppressive business owners to keep the oppressed in their place.

That tax cuts benefit only the rich is the very reason that they are not effective in increasing total spending. The logic is found in something called "propensity to consume." The economically dispossessed have a propensity to consume of 1.0 or greater. This means that the disadvantaged spend at least their entire incomes purchasing those goods and services necessary for life. Tax cuts don't help the oppressed because they pay very little tax to begin with. They save nothing and often go into debt, living "hand to mouth," and payday to payday.

As income increases, propensity to consume, the proportion of current income humyns spend for consumption, decreases. Economic oppressors, friends of conservative government, have propensities to consume of .75 or less. They spend no more than seventy-five percent of their incomes for consumption and save or invest the other twenty-five percent. When the financially privileged receive an effective increase in income through a decrease in taxes, they do not need to purchase more goods and services. They merely increase their savings. Tax cuts will not *force* an increase in total spending, they merely *encourage* such an increase and then only among the wealthy oppressors.

The same is true for investment spending and exports. The government can merely encourage increased investment spending by businesses through lower interest rates. Suppose a capitalist business wants to build a factory that has an expected rate of return of fifteen percent. If money can be borrowed at an interest rate of ten percent, the business will build the factory because a profit of five percent can be made using the money of other capitalist oppressors. If the cost of money is twenty percent, the capitalist will not build the factory because an annual loss of five percent will occur.

Devaluing the dollar on the international market can encourage increases in exports. As an example, take the case of a Nippon sedan imported from Japan. It must be remembered that Japanese capitalists who produce automobiles are paid in yen rather than dollars. When Americans buy a Japanese car, they must first buy yen with which to make the purchase, even though they do not do this directly and likely have no idea that they are doing so. Suppose the Japanese producer is willing and able to sell the car for one million yen. If the exchange rate is two hundred yen for one dollar, as was true in the 1980s, the required yen may be purchased for five thousand dollars. If the price of the dollar falls such that each dollar will purchase only one hundred yen, as was true in the 1990s, then the American purchaser will need ten thousand dollars in order to purchase the required one million yen. Note that the price of the Nippon sedan has not changed! It is the price of money that has changed. The car may be purchased for the same price in Japan, but the price has doubled in the United States. Just the opposite is true for American goods in Japan. When the value of the dollar decreases from two hundred yen per dollar to one hundred, American goods in Japan cost half as much, and Japanese are encouraged to buy more American goods. Exports to Japan and other foreign countries should therefore increase. The key word in the preceding is "encourage." Just as the government cannot force consumers to spend more and business to spend more for investment, it cannot force foreign governments to import more American goods. For a period in the 'eighties, people in Japan didn't want to buy any kind of American car, regardless of price.

The only dimension of total spending over which the government has absolute control is government spending itself. The government can increase its spending during a recession, thereby guaranteeing an increase in total demand. This did in fact happen during the Great Depression, when the alphabet soup of government agencies such as the CCC, WPA and its distant cousin the PWA came into existence under President Franklyn D. Roosevelt's New Deal. This was the most politically correct era of the American economy, when nearly everyone worked for the government and the government was totally responsible for the wellbeing of all American citizens.

The Civilian Conservation Corps was a program under President Franklin D. Roosevelt's New Deal, designed to combat unemployment and poverty. Young men worked for one dollar a day on projects controlling soil erosion, constructing buildings and developing hiking trails in national and state parks. Many of the facilities constructed by the CCC are still in use today. They fought forest fires and planted an estimated three billion trees. Workers lived in camps, were issued uniforms, and were regimented much as the military. They were awakened each morning with a bugle call at six AM and at work by seven forty-five. Because of its excellent work in conservation and the healthy lifestyle of its young workers, the CCC became one of the most popular New Deal programs.

The Public Works Administration employed skilled workers, architects, engineers and artisans to construct public buildings, bridges, dams and housing developments. And they did it magnificently! They constructed 7,488 school buildings and one-third of the hospitals built between 1933 and 1939. Their most famous projects include the Lincoln tunnel, Grand Coulee Dam, and the Key West highway.

The Works Project Administration was a make-work program for unskilled labor. This was the program accused of sending ten workers with one shovel out to dig a hole. I remember my father saying that WPA really stood for "We Piddle Around."

A major benefit to be derived from increased government spending during recessions is that such increases can be directed toward specific sectors of the economy. As pointed out earlier, increases in demand which result from decreases in taxes will be through spending by the economically privileged who will use their newly-found windfall to purchase frivolous luxuries. Tax cuts favor only the rich. When increasing its own spending, a benevolent government can select minority-owned businesses for contract awards, designate spending for urban renewal areas in which the economically oppressed live, or provide direct transfer payments to the economically marginalized or differently motivated. Such selective increases in spending will not only increase total demand by giving the monetary deficient more money to spend, but will contribute to the equality of all.

An increase in spending without an increase in taxes is seen as the ideal fiscal policy to combat recessions. Conservative oppressors of course look upon this with scorn as deficit spending. Such increases in spending supported by printing new money is inflationary, they say. Prices will go up, causing decreases in real wages. Real wages are current wages corrected for inflation. The dollar will become worth less, eroding the income and meager wealth of the oppressed. The politically correct economist does not accept these claims, having seen no proof of their validity.

During a period of inflation, government may decrease total demand by decreasing government spending or increasing taxes, or both. Oppressive conservatives prefer a decrease in government spending because this policy leads to a smaller and less powerful government. Politically correct liberal economists prefer an increase in taxes levied against the privileged classes. Money used by the rich for conspicuous consumption will be transferred to the government, which can in turn transfer the additional revenue to the economically marginalized and those who are owed a living because of past societal transgressions. Conservative economists object to tax increases because of their erroneous belief that taxes, once increased, are never reduced. Taxes therefore get higher and higher, they believe, transferring more spending power from private citizens to the public sector and fostering growth of government. Politically correct economists reject this position because a beneficent government will always reduce the added taxes when the specter of inflation disappears.

Another method of controlling the economy, favored by conservative oppressors and sometimes tolerated by the liberal oppressed, is monetary policy. Interest rates are controlled by changing the money supply. During a recession, the money supply is allowed to increase. Interest rates, the price of money, will decline as will the price of any other commodity as that commodity becomes more plentiful. Lower interest rates are beneficial to the economically marginalized because they can now afford more debt. Consumer durables such as new homes, automobiles, washing machines and even consumer nondurables and services are easier to finance. With lower interest rates, conservatives claim that economic oppressors will build more factories, increasing investment and providing more jobs. American dollars are also cheaper. Prices on American goods overseas will fall and foreigners will clamor for American-made products, increasing exports. The claim of elitist conservative economists is that Gross Domestic Product will rise after a decrease in interest rates, providing economic growth and therefore more jobs for the oppressed. In actuality, more oppression is created in the form of minimum-wage jobs, making products that can be sold at high prices because of lower interest rates. Rich oppressors make more profit and inequality is increased.

During inflation the money supply is decreased. Because money is now scarce, interest rates will rise. This is seen as particularly mean-spirited since the differently advantaged will now be unable to buy homes, automobiles, washing machines and dryers because they cannot afford the higher monthly payments. A one percent increase in interest rates will increase the monthly payment on a $100,000, thirty-year mortgage by seventy-three dollars. The increase in monthly payments will result in a total increase in cost of the home by $27,000 over thirty years. Privileged classes will not be affected because they do not need to make monthly payments in order to purchase these items.

With higher interest rates and the resulting higher investment costs, businesses will not build new factories. Jobs will be taken away from those who really need them, even though these jobs may provide only a subsistence income. Because American dollars are too expensive, foreigners will be unable to buy American goods and exports will decrease. Total spending will decline and inflationary pressures will decrease.

Politically correct economists reject the use of monetary policy as a tool for controlling the economy because all corrections are made through the market, which is an invention of economic oppressors and therefore basically wicked. The government has little control over what will be produced and sold through the market, and corrections made through the market will always benefit the economically privileged who operate it.

The politically correct economist therefore prefers fiscal policy as a tool for maintaining economic stability. Increases in government spending rather than tax cuts should always be used to combat recession. Increases in spending can be targeted to benefit certain groups and to transfer wealth from the privileged classes to those who really deserve it. It is also the position of the politically correct that tax cuts should not be used because THE GOVERNMENT SHOULD NEVER CUT TAXES! Tax cuts can be particularly dangerous to the political correctness movement because ordinary American citizens may become accustomed to them. And, once middle-class householders see the benefits they derive from tax cuts, they may want more of them! Tax cuts could become too popular.

Tax increases, rather than spending decreases, should be used as a defense against inflation. **GOVERNMENT SHOULD NEVER CUT SPENDING!** A decrease in government spending will result in a decrease in government power. A strong central government is essential to the politically correct movement.

Spending increases and tax increases keep economic corrections in the hands of the government. A beneficent Government is in a better position to know what is best for private citizens than are citizens themselves.

136

CH. 11: THE ECONOMIC FUNCTIONS OF GOVERNMENT: REDISTRIBUTION OF INCOME

Demonstrating that he will be run the country with political correctness, President Obama said, "I think when you spread the wealth around it's good for everybody."

Karl Marx saw cycles of recession and inflation as the major problem of capitalism. With each economic cycle, inequality among citizens would increase. The rich would become richer and the poor would become poorer. His thoughts were prophetic. For a brief review, you will recall that inequality in the United States is such that the richest five percent of families receive more than twenty percent of total income. The richest twenty percent receive fifty percent of all income in the United States. On the other end, the poorest twenty percent of families receive less than five percent of income. The distribution of wealth--securities, homes, cars, property--is much more distressing. The wealthiest one percent of families owns more than one-third the total wealth in the United States. The top ten percent owns more than two-thirds. The remaining ninety percent of families own the remaining one-third while the bottom forty percent of the population owns less than one percent.

In 1960 over twenty-two percent of all families in America lived in poverty. In 1963 the architect of the Great Society, Lyndon B. Johnson, declared War on Poverty and by 1965 the proportion of citizens in poverty had decreased to just over seventeen percent. By 1970 the poverty rate had decreased to 12.6 percent. The poverty rate for members of the African Diaspora in 1970, the first year that such data were available, was a whopping 33.5 percent. Since that time, the overall poverty rate has remained steady while the poverty rate for persons of color decreased to twenty-two percent, but since has risen to twenty-five percent. The poverty rate for those of Hispanic origin, first available in 1975, has remained around twenty-five percent.

Inequality and poverty exist for various reasons. First and foremost, the economically marginalized have had no inheritance, the major source of riches for a large proportion of the privileged class. The economically advantaged own ninety percent of all stocks, bonds, business equity, noncommercial real estate, and trusts. When the oppressive rich die, these assets are inherited by their heirs who selfishly refuse to share their newly found riches with the more deserving economically marginalized. What do they do with their newly-found wealth? They spend it foolishly buying cars, boats, SUVs, houses at the beach and in the mountains, light aircraft and, of course, pickup trucks.

The lack of inheritance is one major reason that the economically disadvantaged remain disadvantaged throughout life. Children of privileged economic oppressors inherit mental and physical opportunities that allow them to enter the best schools and subsequent high-paying professions. Children of the economically exploited and people of color have no such inheritance and are seen by elitist educators as differently abled and motivationally deficient. When first entering school they are tagged as "special" students and assigned to education tracks that prepare them for menial and low-paying occupations. Low-income people are then denied the higher education and training provided the privileged classes. Children of the economically marginalized cannot afford the private schools that are the playground of the advantaged child. The disadvantaged often make poor grades throughout their public school careers and cannot gain admission to the finest American universities such as Harvard, Yale and the University of Texas. Even those who finish four years of higher education and hold baccalaureate degrees are often said to not have grades high enough to gain admission to medical and law schools. This is discrimination of the vilest kind. If those with poor grades were offered the opportunity of a medical or law profession, they would be grateful for a second chance, try harder than privileged students and would certainly succeed, even though they may be somewhat grade deficient.

Finally, discrimination is a major cause of inequality and poverty. Wimyn are often able to find work only in low-paying occupations such as secretary or teacher, still considered "female" jobs by oppressive white males. People of color are offered only menial labor jobs, the kind performed by their slave ancestors. Since there is little chance for advancement in these positions, it is highly unlikely that wimyn and people of color will ever move out of poverty.

Regardless of the underlying cause, people live in poverty because they don't have enough money. If income and wealth for all humyns were equal, there would be no poverty.

It is for obvious reasons that the politically correct economist sees the redistribution of wealth and income as the major economic responsibility of government. Each humyn, regardless of ability or motivation, is entitled to an equal share of all goods and services produced by the economy of the United States.

Government can take several approaches to eliminating inequality. Historically, the approach has been to treat the symptoms of inequality through programs of insurance and public assistance. Insurance programs include Social Security, Medicare and Unemployment Insurance. The major problem with so-called social insurance programs is that needy and deserving humyns must first have paid premiums for some minimum period of time in order to qualify for benefits. Premiums are generally taken out of workers' paychecks before the workers receive them. In all cases, government forces oppressive employers to pay all or a portion of the required premiums. And the unfortunate humyn must have suffered the vilest form of oppression—h'orsh' must have worked for meager wages under a capitalist oppressor.

Prior to 1935 there were few, if any, retirement programs for oppressed workers. Those who could

140

afford it bought a kind of postal savings certificates and, if they were willing to take the risk, placed their meager savings in bank savings accounts. Common people did not yet trust banks following the crash of 1929. My father, a woods foreman living in a "company town" owned by a large timber company, told of how he and my mother, after rumors of bank failures, made the trip into town to withdraw their savings of fifty dollars from the local bank and buy my mother a much-needed pair of shoes. The trip was no small task. The distance was about 20 miles over unimproved dirt roads in a 1920s model A Ford. They were too late. By the time they got to the bank, the doors were closed and my mother had no new shoes. He never fully trusted banks again.

On August 14, 1935, President Roosevelt signed HR 7260 and the Old Age and Survivors Income Trust Fund became law. Ostensibly to combat poverty among the aged, the program was designed to encourage workers to retire and make room for unemployed younger workers who needed jobs. With no retirement program, workers would continue working until they died on the job. Congress and the president figured something must be done to provide relief from the twenty-five percent unemployment rate. Social Security tax was at first only one percent of the first $3,000 in wages. In 1950, tax was increased to one and one-half percent of the first $3,600 earned. Medicare was added in 1966 and the combined Medicare and Social Security tax rate increased to 4.2 percent of the first $6,600 earned. Tax rates and the cap, the maximum earnings subject to Social Security tax, continued to increase as the Social Security Trust

Fund flirted with bankruptcy several times during the 1980s and 1990s.

Ida May Fuller was the first recipient of benefits. She retired in 1939 after paying a total of $24.75 in Social Security tax over three years. On January 31, 1940 she received a check for $22.50 and continued to receive benefits for the next thirty-five years. She died in 1975 at the age of one hundred, and had received a total of $22,888.92 in benefits. Ida had realized an annual rate of return of twenty-two percent! The economically oppressed of today should not expect to do that well. It is unlikely that they will receive in total benefits the amount paid in tax.

In order to be "fully insured" for Social Security retirement, survivors or disability benefits, one must have worked a total of ten years. The ten years do not have to be consecutive, but can be three months at a time spread throughout the worker's lifetime. In order to receive disability benefits, one must, in addition to being fully insured, have worked twenty of the forty quarters before becoming disabled.

Premiums for Medicare (hospitalization insurance only) are included in the amount deducted from oppressed workers' paychecks for Social Security contributions. A total of 7.65 percent of earnings before taxes, 6.2 percent for retirement and disability insurance and 1.45 percent for hospitalization insurance, is withheld. The 1.45 percent for hospitalization insurance is certain to increase as the Medicare program encounters bankruptcy during the first half of the twenty-first century. Elderly humyns who are not fully insured may qualify for hospitalization insurance by voluntarily paying a monthly premium. Once a humyn reaches the age of sixty-five, h'orsh' may elect to enroll in a supplemental health insurance program, which pays a portion of outpatient costs. These programs, sold by commercial insurance companies, are grotesquely expensive to oppressed humyns, costing over two hundred dollars a month. The cost is certain to increase in proportion to increases in the cost of medical services.

The Social Security payroll tax is a regressive tax that favors privileged classes because the tax must be paid on only a portion of wages received. A regressive tax requires that lower income earners pay taxes at a higher rate than the wealthy. In 1983, Social Security taxes were paid on only the first $35,700 of income received, $14,000 less than mean household income. The cap on Social Security earnings increased to $94,200 in 2006, but still remains well below the income levels of wealthy oppressors. Humyns earning $94,200 or less must paid Social Security tax at a rate of 7.65 percent. Humyns earning $188,400 annually paid Social Security tax at a rate of only 3.825 percent. The economically deprived were taxed on virtually all of their incomes while only a small portion of the incomes of the advantaged was subject to the Social Security tax. Furthermore, old-age pensions are based on income while working. Those who earned more get higher pensions. This is true even if the retiree is among the super rich and does not need the meager pension. It is obvious that Social Security is a program designed to benefit the economically advantaged.

In order to provide some degree of equity, however, a wise and beneficent government has dictated that oppressive employers match dollar for dollar the contributions of their exploited employees. The overachieving self-employed must pay both the employee and employer's share--a total of 15.3 percent of income before taxes. Even with frequent increases in tax rates and the earnings cap, Social Security is still not completely out of trouble. The Social Security Administration admits that the trust funds will enter bankruptcy in 2042. The Congressional Budget Office predicts bankruptcy ten years later, in 2052.

Social Security unfairly discriminates against the economically oppressed. Because they cannot afford the healthy lifestyle of the advantaged, they do not live long enough to receive benefits sufficient to return even the taxes they have paid into the system. Research by Dr. Robert Banis of the University of Missouri, St. Louis, has indicated that thirty-four percent of those in poverty smoke cigarettes versus a seventeen percent rate for the economically advantaged. This is not the fault of the poor. They simply cannot afford the higher levels of education in which they would learn that smoking is harmful and extremely expensive. The poor are also more likely to dine at fast food outlets and have higher levels of cholesterol and obesity. Because of smoking and unhealthy eating habits, the economically oppressed have limited life expectancies and cannot expect to receive benefits for the same number of years as the advantaged. While this is not good news for those in poverty, it is not all bad for the Social Security Trust Fund. Opinions differ on exactly when the Social Security system will enter bankruptcy, but is sure to happen. Oppressive conservatives want to admit as many oppressed humyns with their limited life expectancy into Social Security as possible. The logic is that, because of their unhealthy life styles, the poor will pay into the system during their working lives and die before receiving many, if any, benefits. More money will then be available to pay the benefits of longer-living oppressors.

Unemployment compensation, created in the Social Security Act of 1935, is an insurance program designed to protect workers who lose their jobs through no fault of their own. Again, the government has benevolently placed the burden of insurance premiums on oppressive employers, who must pay a tax of 6.2 percent on each worker's annual wages. In order to be eligible for benefits, humyns must have worked during the past year and be ready, willing and able to work again.

The major problem with all social insurance programs is that in order to qualify for benefits, a humyn must have worked and paid premiums in the past or, in the case of Medicare, pay a higher premium after retirement. Because of the work requirement, many of the differently abled and motivationally deficient are excluded. Social Insurance programs have therefore done little for the oppressed, but have been of great benefit to what remains of the so-called middle classes.

Public assistance programs, to which privileged white male oppressors refer with disdain as welfare, are open to only the needy. All programs are equitable in that no prior employment or premiums are required. One must only pass the appropriate means test--that is, one must have an income and assets less than a predetermined amount. Welfare programs are more equitable than insurance programs because anyone with income below the government-established poverty level, regardless of the reason, is eligible for assistance. Public assistance can be in the form of cash payments or "in-kind" assistance.

Not too long ago, the best-known and most successful forms of public assistance was Aid to Families with Dependent Children (AFDC), in which cash payments were given directly to economically marginalized parents. AFDC was first authorized under the Social Security Act of 1935 as a joint Federal-state program to assist needy families. While most of the money to finance the program came from the Federal government, individual states were designated responsible for administration of the program. Benefits therefore varied unfairly from state to state.

AFDC was one of the favorite targets of criticism by mean-spirited conservatives who liked to refer to AFDC as the "welfare baby program," insinuating that many wimyn had babies merely to receive more income from our benevolent government. Republicans liked to point out meaningless facts, such as the number of families receiving AFDC payments increasing at a rate four times faster than the total number of families in the country. These and other criticisms led to calls for welfare reform by the oppressive elite who had never been in need of public assistance. Even the Great Benefactor, President Bill Clinton, declared in order to be elected that he would "...end welfare as we know it."

The Welfare Reform Law, or Personal Responsibility and Work Opportunity Reconciliation Act of 1996, replaced AFDC and other job training programs with Temporary Assistance for Needy Families (TANF). It is obvious that oppressive conservative politicians designed TANF because the differently motivated are expected to work. This has led to the term "welfare" being replaced by the term "workfare." Benefit recipients who cannot find meaningful employment are assigned work tasks by oppressive politicians, tasks which are supposed to prepare the economically oppressed for entry into the world of work. In reality, public assistance recipients have been assigned tasks such as scrubbing sidewalks or picking up trash left on the streets by the oppressive rich. The accomplishment of these menial tasks will hardly prepare for future jobs in the business world those who are now ill prepared for any kind of productive work. The economically oppressed are further penalized because benefit payments are limited to a period of five years.

Because TANF is administered by individual states, benefits are unfairly distributed. In New Mexico, one of our poorest states with a poverty rate of over 17.3 percent in 2004, a family received an average of $630 a month. In close runner-up Arkansas, with a poverty rate of 16.4 percent, an average family received only $345. Neither of these amounts is enough to meet monthly needs. In Connecticut, which has a poverty rate of only nine percent, the average family receives $1,750! While this amount does not allow an oppressed family to live a life of luxury, it does allow them to retain some dignity.

The second major form of cash payment to the differently abled and motivationally deficient is Supplemental Security Income (SSI). This program, established by the Federal Government in the 1972 Social Security Act Amendments, provides cash payments to the blind, disabled and elderly. The major advantage of SSI is the interpretation of "disabled" by our wise government. Those who are addicted to drugs or alcohol may qualify for benefits, but will have to undergo treatment in order to qualify in the future. It is not necessary that they be cured of their addiction. Addicts have received SSI benefits even though Congress in 1996 passed a law denying benefits for drug addicts. Benevolent judges have granted benefits because addicts who could not complete rehab programs were not sober enough to work. The only requirement seems to be that the addict must not have been convicted of a drug felony.

Parents of students who are classified as "disruptive" by their schools may be entitled to a cash payment, as disruption can be interpreted as a disability. The most desirable aspect of SSI is that it can eliminate the need for oppressed American residents to be financially responsible for themselves or their families and can increase household income.

"In-kind" assistance consists of specific services provided to the economically marginalized who are receiving either or both TANF and SSI payments. Those who need medical care are provided that care by the government under

Medicaid. Those who need food are provided vouchers, known as food stamps, with which to buy food. Housing subsidies for builders and vouchers for renters provide housing for those who for whatever reasons do not have resources to purchase or rent their own housing. WIC (Women, Infants and Children) is a nutrition program for oppressed wimyn and their children. Milk, cereal, peanut butter, diapers and other items required by the child or mother are available through the program. Such payments make it possible for the economically oppressed to own other goods, such as automobiles which are not provided by the government and otherwise only the advantaged classes could own. In-kind assistance frees money received through TANF and SSI so it can be used to purchase these otherwise unobtainable items.

The Welfare Laws of 1996 and other actions by oppressive conservatives in government have denied the differently motivated and differently abled their right to luxuries that are readily available to themselves and other economic oppressors. Before the oppressive 1996 Welfare Laws, the average oppressed beneficiary received seventeen thousand dollars annually. This was only three thousand dollars less than the income of the average production worker in the United States, about the average first-year salary for a teacher in many states, and $7,120 more than a worker making minimum wage would earn working forty hours a week for a year. This provided only a little dignity for those who did not work because of poor health or different motivation, because it was still $8,500 less than median income. The Cato Institute found in a 1996 study that the total package of welfare benefits ranged from a high of $36,400 in Hawaii to a low of $11,500 in Mississippi.

An obvious way to bring about equality and dignity among all is to attack and correct some of the reasons for inequality. As stated earlier, those who are offspring of the privileged have a head start on the economically deprived, while those who are born in poverty usually remain in poverty. One reason is that as children of the economically oppressed enter the first grade of school, they are often told that they are poor and are not expected to do well. Teachers will do all they can to help, they say, but they also say that the student should really not expect to be successful. Younger students are often evaluated when they enter school and are then divided into study groups named after cute birds. There are bluebirds, redbirds and buzzards. Guess which are in the buzzards group. Those who are poor and are not really expected to do well. The self-fulfilling prophecy then takes over--they don't do well.

The government has tried to bring about more equality of children through the Head Start preschool program, in which children are taught at a very young age the social skills necessary for success in kindergarten and elementary school. This program has not been very successful, perhaps because previously learned inappropriate habits are too ingrained to overcome.

There is only one solution to the problem: If all were equal at birth, then all would have an equal opportunity and incentive to succeed. Unequal, however, would be the means of success. In order

150

for means to be equal, inheritances would have to be equal.

In a politically correct economy inheritances would be redistributed to the deserving economically disadvantaged through an increased and strictly enforced estate tax. This would immediately transfer the inheritance to the government for later redistribution to the poor. A tax of one hundred percent is recommended to totally eliminate the deleterious effects of obscene inheritances and to place all on a more equal initial economic footing.

It may be impossible to alter inherent ability differences. However, offspring of the economically advantaged and disadvantaged may be made more equal in ability by placing them in the same environment at a very early age. Common day and night care centers for children of different abilities should be established. It may be necessary for government to force the economically advantaged to place their children in these centers. Music and dance lessons for the rich will be prohibited unless similar lessons are provided for all. Soccer and gymnastics moms will gladly, for the sake of equality, fill their vans with the underprivileged and economically oppressed as they transport their own children to these activities.

Strong affirmative action programs should be established and enforced to ensure that the economically marginalized, differently abled and differently motivated are admitted to schools and occupations that have been previously closed to the disadvantaged. To admit students to law and medical colleges on the basis of academic preparation and grade point average is a wicked form of discrimination. The oppressed are excluded under such policies simply because they have not had the same educational opportunities afforded the privileged classes. While a quota system for professional education is not recommended, a wise and benevolent government should ensure that there is equal representation of the economically deprived and differently motivated who, when given this opportunity, will certainly prevail and become exemplars of professional society.

Market intervention has been used with only limited success to bring about more equality. Training programs are designed to improve skills of workers and therefore increase their value, which leads to higher wages. Republican conservatives criticize job-training programs because they are too expensive and students often do not finish their training. The real problem is that once students finish training, there are no jobs to be had. Job training programs are therefore ineffective unless the government simultaneously creates jobs.

A very effective market intervention technique to bring about more equality is a minimum wage law. Such laws are politically controversial, but the politically correct see them as an acceptable way to force business owners to pay a fairer wage to their oppressed employees. An increase in minimum wages will increase worker morale because workers will feel more valuable. Employers will also use their workers more efficiently at the higher wage rate.

Republican oppressors oppose minimum wage laws because, they say, higher unemployment results from such laws. For example, suppose an employer has twelve dollars an hour with which to pay workers. If the minimum wage is three dollars an hour, the employer will hire four workers. If the minimum wage is increased to four dollars an hour, the employer will be able to hire only three workers and one will be fired. They try to prove their claim by pointing to increases in unemployment after each minimum wage increase. It is also claimed that increases in wages will cause producers to replace workers with technology. The politically correct economist does not accept this claim as valid. Increases in unemployment that have occurred after minimum wages are increased could have easily been caused by other factors.

Another objection of conservatives to minimum wages is that they are supposedly inflationary. It is true that greedy owners of businesses will pass increases in wages and other costs of production to consumers. Stronger government regulation is needed to control prices and prevent the passing of increases in production costs on to consumers.

Minimum wage laws have been somewhat ineffective. This is largely because workers paid prescribed minimum wages still have incomes that are below the poverty level. At $5.15 an hour, the rate established by the Federal government in 1997 and still in effect in 2006, an employee working full time will receive only $206 weekly, $10,712 annually if no vacation is taken. This is over twenty thousand dollars less than median household income and is not a livable wage. Prices have increased twenty-five percent since 1997, making current minimum wage even more inadequate. It would have to be increased to $6.50 just to keep up with inflation. A minimum wage of ten dollars an hour would provide an income of twenty thousand dollars a year, which would have placed minimum wage earners close to, but not quite in, middle class in 1997 but not in 2006. Even better, the minimum wage should be established at fifteen dollars an hour, providing an annual income of thirty thousand dollars and then adjusted annually for inflation. This would place all workers at or near the median income level, providing a great incentive for those now on public assistance to seek employment. The greatest benefit is that no one would exist at or below the poverty level since all would have incomes above the median. All government poverty programs could be eliminated, resulting in an immediately balanced budget. The House of Representatives continues to support increases in minimum wage but are resisted by the oppressive Senate. Republicans in the Senate in 2007, after tax concessions by House Democrats, did agree to an increase in minimum wage to $7.25 an hour over two years. This amount will place a family of two at or slightly above the expected poverty level in 2009 but well below the median income level and is therefore unacceptable.

The problem common to all programs of public assistance is that once a beneficiary obtains work, his or her benefits begin to disappear. Humyns are therefore discouraged from obtaining work and becoming independent. Instead of penalizing those who are among the economically marginalized because of ability or motivation, but are still ambitious, the government should reward them for seeking work. Humyns who are receiving welfare payments and obtain work should receive, in addition to their new incomes, additional welfare benefits from the government. Working welfare recipients will therefore have higher incomes, both in wages and increased benefits, than those who don't work.

In a particularly mean-spirited move, a Republican-dominated Congress in 1996 pushed through the welfare reform law that now requires recipients to work after receiving public assistance for two years. The law also allows states to deny additional benefits to wimyn who have another child while receiving welfare. The stated purpose is to get humyns off the welfare roles and encourage them to work. This is in direct opposition to the responsibility of the government to establish and maintain an equal distribution of income. Most humyns on welfare are unable to perform any type of productive work. Those who are differently abled or have motivation deficiencies will be forced off the welfare roles. The measure of success in any system of redistribution of income must be the number of those receiving benefits.

Until a beneficent government transfers wealth and income from the economically advantaged to all oppressed humyns, equality cannot exist. The capitalistic economic system, in which workers are paid on the basis of their contribution to total production, has not succeeded in bringing about equality of income. As long as the profit motive is supreme, inequality will only become more egregious. Now- severe oppression of the economically marginalized will become even more severe.

CH.12: HOW TO FINANCE EQUALITY: FEDERAL TAXES

Oliver Wendell Holmes once said, "Taxes are what we pay for a civilized society," a statement that is inscribed at the entrance to the Internal Revenue Building in Washington, D.C. We may also say that taxes are what a politically correct society pays to bring about equality among all, for it is only by transferring wealth from the elite rich to the differently abled and motivationally deficient that true equality can be attained. The major purpose of any system of taxation must be to bring about equality among all humyns.

Major considerations by any government in establishing a fair system of taxes are progressivity (or regressivity), and how the tax burden is apportioned among the populace. Progressive taxes are favored over regressive taxes by the politically correct because the rich pay a higher tax rate than the poor and destitute. It is important to note that progressivity or regressivity refers to tax RATE, not the absolute amount in dollars of tax paid. The best example of a progressive tax is, of course, the progressive income tax, because that is what the name says it is. A regressive tax requires that the poor pay a higher tax rate than the rich. This is particularly mean-spirited and is favored by rich economic oppressors. A proportional, or flat rate, tax is one in which all taxpayers pay taxes at the same rate. It should be made clear at this time that the emphasis is on tax RATE, not absolute taxes. In a regressive tax, the poor may be paying less tax than the rich but still be paying at a higher rate, thereby bearing a greater tax burden.

Tax burdens are generally apportioned among the various taxpayers by one of two methods: ability to pay or benefits received. The best example of ability to pay is again the progressive income tax, in which the rich are required to pay tax at a higher rate than the poor. Those who are rich and able pay tax at a higher rate than the oppressed and unable. Taxes paid under the benefits received principle are often called use taxes and include tolls for the use of roads and bridges, gasoline taxes for the privilege of driving one's car on state and Federal roads, fees for the use of public boat ramps to launch private fishing boats, and property taxes to support schools, police and fire departments. Both methods of apportionment have their problems. Who actually has the ability to pay exorbitant taxes levied by corrupt politicians? Do the poor have the ability to pay excessive progressive income taxes required by some governments? Who actually receives the benefit from so-called use taxes? What about the economically oppressed humyn who buys gasoline for his small outboard motor? He plans only to catch a few fish to feed his hungry family, but must pay a highway "use tax" to buy fuel for his small boat that will never cruise down a state road.

How does each of the common taxes levied by Federal, state and local governments comply with the above characteristics? Close examination will reveal that these characteristics are nothing more than economic balderdash. First take the best known of all taxes, the progressive income tax. This tax is, of course, progressive because rich economic oppressors are supposed to pay their tax at a higher rate than the poor oppressed. And the name says that the tax is progressive. True? There are all sorts of loopholes available to capitalist oppressors, loopholes that are not available to the average proletariat. First is the privilege of home ownership. Interest payments on mortgages up to one million dollars are deductible in their entirety. This would enable one of the oppressively rich to deduct up to seventy thousand dollars in income during the first year of hi'r mansion ownership. While a mortgage deduction is available to the average oppressed humyn for hi'r measly mortgage, not many can afford a million dollar plus mansion.

Another loophole available to the oppressively rich involves tax-deferred savings. There is a hodgepodge of plans including 401(k)s, 403(b)s, SIMPLES (Savings Incentive Match Plans for Employees), IRAs, 401(k)s, Roth IRAs and so forth. Probably the most familiar of these is the latter, the Roth IRA. Contributions to the Roth IRA, unlike the old IRA, are not tax deductible but all the earnings resulting from such a plan ARE TAX FREE! Younger workers can invest as much as four thousand dollars a year and those over fifty years of age can invest an additional thousand bucks. Not a plan for the oppressed proletariat! Humyns must have loose money lying around in order to participate. Again, this is a loophole to benefit rich oppressors.

158

Capital gains on investments is another loophole available only to rich oppressors who can afford to invest in the first place. Returns on investment in stocks and real estate are currently taxed by the Federal government at a rate of only fifteen percent. Data from The Tax Foundation show that seventy-five percent of taxpayers over sixty years of age, those of the population who can afford to invest, claim capital gains on their annual income taxes while only twenty-three percent of those under the age off thirty-five do! The young who are differently abled or motivationally challenged are penalized by oppressive governments for their inability to invest in lucrative schemes developed by equally oppressive bankers. The same tax system that requires a person making over one hundred thousand dollars a year to pay only fifteen percent of capital gains on Federal income tax requires that a poor family of two with only five dollars taxable income pay one dollar in tax, a rate of twenty percent! Worse yet, a couple with taxable income of $12,830, the poverty level in 2005 under an oppressive Republican president, would pay $1,283 in Federal income tax. A rate of only ten percent, but enough to place the oppressed working family $1,283 below the poverty level!

State income taxes place additional burdens on the economically oppressed. In the state of West Virginia, with one of the highest poverty levels in the United States, a family of four with an annual income of ten thousand dollars, half the Federally established poverty level, must begin paying state income tax, driving the family further into poverty. A family of four in Hawaii with an income of only $11,500 must pay some state income tax.

The state sales tax is a particularly mean-spirited tax levied by all but five states. Naive politicians consider the sales tax a progressive tax because they assume that those who earn more will spend more, which is in fact true. They also consider it a fair tax because humyns don't have to buy things if they don't want to pay the tax, which is not true. I once heard a local politician say, "What we need is a local option sales tax because that's the fairest tax there is." The sales tax is in fact the unfairest tax of all because it is the most regressive. The poor pay a much higher tax rate than the rich. Sales taxes are consumption taxes and all humyns, rich and poor, must consume. The problem with consumption taxes is that the poor spend a larger proportion of their income for consumption than the rich. An example is obvious. Consider an oppressed humyn working for a barely subsistence wage of only ten thousand dollars a year, even after the wage is reduced by mean-spirited governments through their oppressive income tax. This economically marginalized humyn will spend the entire ten thousand just existing. In an area where many economically advantage live, such as Gulf Shores, Alabama where the combined state and local sales taxes total nine percent, the economically oppressed humyn will pay a tax rate of nine percent because all of hi'r income is taxed! Now consider the marginally advantaged humyn who has an income of one hundred thousand dollars a year or more. That humyn may choose to live sparingly and spend only ten thousand dollars annually and be taxed at a rate of only nine-tenths of one percent. The most likely case is that the economically advantaged humyn will choose to consume about fifty thousand dollars annually. In this case h'orsh' will pay $4,500 in taxes, resulting in a tax rate of 4.5 percent, half that of the economically oppressed humyn. The economic oppressor will then have $45,500 to invest in capital gains loopholes and become even richer.

Another tax that unfairly penalizes the poor and oppressed is the state gasoline tax. Politicians consider gasoline taxes a user fee because gasoline tax funds are dedicated to transportation and highway systems. They are in fact consumption or sales taxes and are therefore regressive. The Federal gasoline tax in 2005 was 18.4 cents per gallon. State gasoline taxes ranged from less than ten cents to over thirty-three cents per gallon, with an average of about twenty-two cents. The smallest is in Georgia at 7.5 cents per gallon; the largest is in New York at 33.55 cents per gallon. The tax is regressive because the poor use as much or more gasoline as the rich and therefore pay a larger portion of their income for the tax. The oppressed also cannot afford newer fuel-efficient hybrid cars that the rich buy daily. They require more fuel to drive their older gas burners to work and to the grocery store.

And finally there is the local property tax, which supports schools, police, fire protection, statues of local politicians and any other project dear to city and county fathers. This is a fair, progressive tax, say economic oppressors, because the rich live in bigger houses in more expensive parts of town and therefore pay more taxes. This is true. However, the poor spend a larger portion of their meager income for housing and this makes the tax regressive, with the poor paying a higher tax rate. But, the rich say, most of the poor do not own homes. They rent their places to live and therefore pay no property tax. What we are talking about here is tax incidence, or who finally pays the tax. In this case, the oppressive landlord passes the tax on to the renter in the rental payment. The oppressed renter is the one who finally pays the tax.

It is obvious that the tax structure in the United States punishes the economically oppressed. So what must be done? There have been several movements toward tax reform, the most popular of which include value added tax, flat tax and the so-called "fair tax."

The value added tax is nothing more than a hidden sales tax and is therefore regressive, as are all consumption taxes. The tax is paid by producers, hidden in the price of the product and ultimately passed on to the consumer. An example used in economics textbooks is a woolen sports jacket. The cost and value added at each stage of production from purchasing the wool from the sheepherder to manufacture to final sales are totaled. But only capitalist economic oppressors wear woolen sports jackets made by companies such as Mark, Shuffler and Harx. Our example is leather work boots, worn daily by oppressed laborers all over America.

Assume an added value tax of ten percent. The following is an example of how the tax would work.

162

Product	Value	Added	Tax	Selling Price
Cowhide	4.00	4.00	.40	4.40
Leather	10.00	6.00	.60	11.00
Boots	100.00	90.00	9.00	110.00

Suppose the cattle rancher or meat packing plant sells enough cowhide to make one pair of boots to the leather maker for four dollars. The rancher or packing company has added a value of four dollars to nothing and must pay the government forty cents in tax. The rancher or meat packer will add the tax to the selling price of the leather and will charge the leather maker $4.40. The leather maker tans the hide to make leather that has a value of ten dollars, but must be sold to the boot maker for eleven dollars in order to recover the tax paid by the leather producer and passed to the boot maker, and the boot maker's own VAT. The added value is now six dollars, which means the leather producer must pay sixty cents to the government. The Foxerine Boot Company now turns the leather into a pair of steel-toe work boots that have a value of one hundred dollars and an added value of ninety dollars, requiring a VAT payment to the government of nine dollars. The price to the oppressed construction worker must be $110 to recover all costs of manufacturing and value added taxes of an otherwise one hundred dollar pair of work boots. This may have been a little confusing, but it is important to note that the incidence of the tax is on the consumer, the one who finally pays the tax, and the tax is therefore a consumption tax.

All consumption and sales taxes are regressive because the poor and oppressed must spend a greater proportion of their meager income just to live. The poor are taxed at a higher rate and this is not acceptable to the politically correct.

Another approach to tax reform has been the flat rate income tax. A flat rate tax is neither regressive nor progressive but proportional in that humyns of all income levels pay the tax at the same rate. Rich economic oppressors like flat taxes because, they say, the rich are not punished for their success. Steve Forbes advocated a flat tax in his 1996 and 2000 presidential campaigns. Congressman Dick Armey introduced a flat tax in the Freedom and Fairness Restoration Acts of 1999 and 2001. His plan would have replaced the current Federal Income tax with a seventeen percent tax rate on income for individuals. A married couple could deduct a personal allowance of $26,200 and an additional $5,300 for each dependent. A family of four could therefore earn $36,800 before paying any income tax. The problem with this tax is that it is a proportional tax that does not allow for redistribution of income, which should be the primary purpose of any taxing system. Another major problem is that, other than the personal exemptions, the tax does not allow for the ability-to-pay principle of apportioning the tax burden. Rich oppressive families are taxed at the same rate as struggling middle class families. Armey's plan is unacceptable to the politically correct.

Steve Forbes' proposal was essentially the same as Dick Armey's. The tax would be seventeen percent and would exempt income for a family of four up to $36,000. He would eliminate tax on social security, pensions, personal savings and capital gains. This plan is unacceptable for the same reasons stated above.

A current movement toward tax reform is the so-called "fair tax." This is not the first time that the term "fair" has been used. Congressman Kemp of Buffalo Bills football fame, and Senator Kasten of no particular fame, proposed in 1985 a "Fair and Simple Tax," which was a flat-rate income tax of twenty-four percent. Kemp was a member of the duo that engineered the 1981 Kemp-Roth Act, the thirty percent tax cut desired by President Reagan. Today's version of the fair tax is a tax on spending, otherwise known as a sales or consumption tax. The fair tax would replace all current Federal income and payroll taxes with a "progressive" national sales tax. No Federal taxes would be deducted from a worker's paycheck. A unique feature of the plan provides a monthly payment, called a "prebate," to each household to cover the tax on expenditures up to the poverty level. This is to ensure that no family would pay the sales tax on necessities and is supposed to make the tax progressive. The tax would be on everything purchased new--food, clothing, medicine, new homes and all services including those of doctors and lawyers. Used goods such as previously owned cars and existing homes would not be taxed. Hidden taxes such as income taxes paid by producers and passed on to consumers would be eliminated because there would be no income tax. Prices paid by consumers for finished products would decrease by the same amount, an amount approximating the fair tax. Presumably, the price of products with fair tax added would be no higher than the price before the fair tax. Theoretically, consumers would effectively pay no tax compared with the current tax system and would benefit from the prebate!   In theory, then, all taxpayers should support implementation of the Fair Tax with enthusiasm!

An advantage emphasized by advocates of the fair tax is that there would be no loopholes. Everyone who has income over the poverty level would pay tax as they spend their money. This includes tax dodgers and illegal aliens who take advantage of the welfare system but pay no taxes. Finally, all visitors and tourists to the United States would pay Federal tax on any and all purchased or consumed goods, which they presently do not do. But the primary benefit, say fair tax advocates, is that we could abolish the Internal Revenue Service, seen by many as the defacto Gestapo of the United States.

But the informed politically correct do not see the fair tax as the panacea it is claimed to be. First, there is no such thing as a progressive sales tax. There is some point at which all sales taxes become regressive. Even after the prebate, a family of four making thirty-five thousand a year, more than ten thousand dollars less than the median family income in the United States, will spend a greater proportion of its above-poverty-level income than a family making two hundred thousand dollars. The prebate must be considered income, which because of the propensity to consume of the poor, oppressed humyns will spend and pay taxes on. The less-than-median income family will pay the "fair" tax at a greater rate than the rich family. Other potential problems abound. Fair tax advocates consist mostly of oppressive rich conservatives and libertarians. It is highly unlikely that they would support elimination of an income tax that allows them to take advantage of the many loopholes.

It is more likely that the fair tax would be in addition to the current Federal income tax. Any crises would require that the Federal income tax be temporarily revived and, as Senator Everett Dirkson once said, "There is nothing more permanent than a temporary government program." Another problem would be inflation. As prices go up, so would Federal taxes causing poorer middle class families to become even poorer. Since used items are not taxed, increased demand for used cars and existing homes would drive prices up. The oppressed middle class could no longer afford an existing home. Higher prices on used items would levy extreme penalties on the on the economically oppressed. Those below the poverty level could no longer afford a now more expensive used car. Higher prices on existing homes would cause increases in rents, even on hovels in which many of the oppressed must live. It is also very doubtful that oppressive capitalist producers will decrease prices to consumers just because they no longer have to pay business taxes. Producers may make a token price reduction but it is more likely that prices will remain at the pre-fair tax level and the "Fair Tax" will be added to whatever price the market will bear.

Finally, since the monthly prebate payment is administered by the Social Security Administration, there are those, including illegal aliens and some religions who do not believe in social security numbers, who do not have legal social security cards and would not receive the monthly prebate. They would therefore have to pay the excessive national sales tax without receiving any compensation from the government. Even if it were not for the problems described above, the "fair tax" and other tax reform schemes discussed previously would not contribute to the redistribution of income from the economically advantaged to the economically marginalized. For this reason, the politically correct reject the "fair tax," flat tax, and value added taxes as being unfair to the economically marginalized.

The only fair tax is the progressive income tax because of its adherence to the ability to pay principle of taxation and its suitability for redistribution of income. But the current Federal income tax is unacceptable as it is now structured. Changes must be made. One redeeming feature of the current income tax is the earned income credit that can mean a tax credit of up to $4,400 for a worker with two children. The credit returns a portion of tax paid by the worker and even can produce a payment to workers who paid no taxes. A problem is that the forms are rather complicated and the economically oppressed do not have the skills to complete them nor the money to hire professional help.

The purpose of taxation is to bring about equality among all. The new great benefactor of humynity Barack Obama made a feeble attempt to provide some relief to the oppressed in his economic stimulus package of 2009 by recommending a tax rebate for oppressed citizens who did not make enough money to pay any taxes at all. To finance this payment, he would increase taxes on all those making more than $250,000 annually. This feeble attempt to bring about some measure of equality was far from sufficient.

The politically correct recommend a negative income tax that would provide a payment to each family member earning less than a predetermined amount. While the earned income credit is like a negative income tax program, it is insufficient to provide needed relief to the economically marginalized. The negative income tax was suggested by economist Milton Friedman as a replacement for the American welfare system. It would have provided a payment from the government to bring families below the subsistence level to a predetermined level of income. Such a move would have perhaps taken families out of poverty but still have left them poor and in a state of extreme inequality.

The politically correct recommend a progressive income tax on all those with incomes above the median. Those with incomes below the median would pay no Federal income tax. The government would take in tax, from the economically advantaged, all income above the median. Tax revenue would then be used to finance payments to the economically marginalized to bring their incomes to the median. A state of economic equality would exist because all humyns would exist at the median income level. The politically correct believe the economically advantaged would readily agree to such a program because the need for expensive welfare programs would be completely eliminated. Welfare programs cost taxpayers in the United States over 666 billion dollars in 2005. Many religious humyns consider 666 the sign of the devil.

CH.13: THE HOMELESS

No one really knows how many homeless humyns there are in the United States. This is not surprising since people who have no address are not counted in the decennial census.

It is also true that intellectual elitists who count the homeless differ in their definitions of exactly who the homeless are. Some are literal in their definitions, counting only those who are currently in shelters, on the streets or in homeless camps. According to this definition, somewhere between three hundred thousand and six hundred thousand people are homeless each night. This amount differs from estimates by advocates for the homeless. Mitch Snyder, a homeless advocate of the 1970s and 1980s, estimated that between 1.5 and three million people were homeless on any given night. We give more credence to this latter figure because all of the homeless are not in shelters, on the streets or in camps. It is highly doubtful that those who count the homeless would actually enter neighborhoods where the homeless are on the streets or "hobo jungles" where the homeless camp. Their data are more likely to be estimates than actual counts. Whatever the actual count, it is estimated that the homeless rate is increasing by at least five percent each year. The rate increases even more as oppressed homeowners become homeless as oppressive bankers foreclose on those who cannot make their mortgage payments.

It is impossible to accurately determine the number of homeless at the start of 2009 because of the subprime mortgage crisis. Many oppressed homebuyers were evicted from their homes when they could not make the monthly payments required when the interest on their adjustable-rate mortgages increased to usurious rates.

Under pressure from the benevolent Clinton administration Fannie Mae, the government-sponsored mortgage underwriter and the largest of its kind in the nation, in 1999 relaxed credit requirements on loans it would purchase from banks and other lenders. This resulted in increased mortgage loan availability for minority and low-income borrowers so that they could finally realize the American dream of home ownership. Attainment of the dream for the economically oppressed was further made possible by Congressman Barney Frank, who has experienced social oppression because of his sexual orientation and can empathize with the economically oppressed as no one else in the Federal government can. Oppressive capitalists and Republicans in Congress continued to express concern that Fannie Mae and its distant cousin Freddie Mac were purchasing mortgage loans made to people who could not pay them back and that the two should receive more oversight. Congressman Frank, in defense of oppressed homeowners, said that their concern was overblown and he "did not regard Fannie Mae and Freddy Mac as problems."

Oppressive lenders who convinced oppressed homebuyers to assume mortgages that were beyond their means to repay caused the problem. They were offered adjustable rate mortgages with very low initial interest rates and were convinced that they could resell the houses at great profit before the rates increased. The collapse of the housing market in 2007 put an end to the dreams of the poor oppressed who thought they could finally experience home ownership. Greedy lenders fraudulently convinced oppressed humyns to purchase homes they couldn't afford. The politically correct see this as a failure of the market system, exacerbating the problem of homelessness in the United States.

Other definitions of the homeless are more liberal and rightly include as homeless the economically marginalized who live in slum areas and spend over half their incomes for substandard housing. Their positions are so precarious that they could be homeless at any time. The number in this group is estimated to be as many as seven million people.

Some sociologists include in their count all those who have been homeless at any time during the last few years. This group has been estimated to be as high as ten million people.

Left out are those who temporarily live with relatives or friends, but have no permanent homes of their own. This group includes differently motivated white males who move in with their vaginal friends in order to obtain free food and shelter. Members of this group are so insecure in their housing arrangements that they too could become homeless at any time. No one knows how large this group is, but it is likely to consist of another ten million humyns. Others are adult children, generally differently motivated nonvaginal humyns who still live with, or have moved back in with, their nondifferently motivated parents.

Current estimates of the number of homeless therefore range from 300,000 to over twenty million oppressed humyns. The actual number of homeless is much greater than that.

Studies by sociologists have provided more enlightenment about the homeless. A 2001 study found that forty-one percent of the urban homeless population was men and fourteen percent was wimyn. A 2003 survey found that forty percent of the homeless consisted of families and thirty-nine percent were children. Another 2003 survey revealed a shocking statistic: sixty-five percent of the homeless were of non-Caucasian ethnicity.

Because of the high proportion of people of color in the homeless population, it is obvious that the leading cause of homelessness in the United States is economic oppression. People are homeless simply because they cannot afford housing. There is therefore a strong and inverse relationship between homelessness and income. Homeless humyns in the United States are primarily those in poverty. Those who are in poverty cannot afford food, clothing, health care and housing.

Economics is a science of choices. When the oppressed of America make their choices, health care and housing get a very low priority. This should not be surprising because housing costs take an ever-increasing proportion of our income. In 1975, those who were fortunate enough to own a home, or at least co-own a home along with an oppressive mortgage lender, paid eighteen percent of their incomes on their mortgages. In 1993, mortgage payments consumed twenty-two percent of income. The typical mortgage payment today is over eight hundred dollars and increases as the price of homes increases. Even homeowners without mortgages, a group which consists of those with extreme economic advantage, pay over ten percent or their income in housing expenses. Those who occupy rental units pay thirty percent of their incomes for housing. In 2005, the median price of a home in the United States approached $250,000! Assuming the standard down payment of twenty percent, the monthly payment on a thirty-year, $200,000 mortgage at six percent annually will be $1,199.10. It is no wonder that the economically disadvantaged comprise the majority of the homeless.

Humyns have continued to be economically disadvantaged because the government has not been responsible in bringing about income equality. Trillions of dollars have been spent in attempts to end poverty since 1963, when a wise and benevolent President Lyndon Johnson declared the Great War on Poverty. Yet the poverty rate remains at about thirteen percent of our population, nearly forty million people. The reason is that even with welfare benefits, oppressed humyns remain below the poverty level. Temporary Assistance to Needy Families provided a maximum monthly benefit for a single-parent family of three of only $170 a month in Mississippi, but increased to $709 for the economically oppressed in Vermont. Payments are not sufficient in either state and increases have not kept up with inflation. Persons fortunate enough to occupy rental units must pay five hundred dollars or more a month to greedy capitalist property owners. The differently abled and motivationally challenged still have incomes below the poverty level, even after including such in-kind aid as Medicaid and food stamps. The incomes of those in poverty just aren't enough to purchase adequate housing.

Another area in which the government has fallen short in its responsibility to the disadvantaged is one we discussed previously-- minimum wage. Minimum wage is insufficient to lift the economically marginalized out of poverty. A minimum wage of $7.25 an hour provides an income of $15,080 a year if no vacation is taken--an income well below the poverty level for a family of four. As recommended earlier, a minimum wage of fifteen dollars an hour would provide an annual wage of over thirty thousand dollars. Even at this income level, a family could not afford a home at today's prices, but might be able to take a vacation and have at least some dignity.

The government has failed the economically marginalized by not providing adequate affordable housing. Because of the mean-spirited policies of conservative politicians, there is a shortfall of millions of low-cost housing units for the differently abled and differently motivated. Between 1980 and 1988, budget authority for all Federal housing programs was cut by eighty-two percent. Over two hundred thousand Federal housing units were authorized from 1977 to 1981, but less than forty-five thousand were authorized under the Reagan administration.

In futile attempts to defend Reagan's actions, conservatives contend that from 1980 to 1989 housing subsidies paid directly to low income families nearly tripled, going from just over five billion to nearly fourteen billion dollars. They also point out that the number receiving housing assistance increased by over one billion families. This is, of course, the approach used by conservative politicians, which places housing subsidies in the private sector rather than the public sector. It is well established that beneficent government agencies are better equipped to develop and manage housing and rental units than are profit-oriented entrepreneurs of the private sector.

Under 2006 budget proposals, 375,000 families may lose housing subsidies as one-third of the block grant program is transferred from the Department of Housing and Urban Development to the Department of Commerce. Will the Department of Commerce, which is primarily interested in the business sector, sympathize with the unfortunate who for many reasons do not work for oppressive businesses? HUD did, however, appropriate $11.5 billion for housing assistance to hurricane Katrina victims.

The politically correct position is that the plight of the homeless is actually much worse than the government is willing to admit. As noted previously, the primary cause of homelessness in the United States is poverty. People are homeless simply because they cannot afford to own a home. A little simple math tells the true story.

Remember that the bottom twenty percent of income earners in the United States receive less than five percent of total income. This means that about sixty million people have a combined annual income of about $450 billion, or an average of about $7,500 each. The figures are for 2005, but since real income has been declining since the 1970s, the situation today will be even worse. Sixty million people, twenty percent of the population of the United States, have average incomes that are less than the poverty level. Of these sixty million economically oppressed who do have homes, their housing situation is so precarious that they are likely to be homeless at any time. This group should be included in any definition of homeless.

The number of homeless in America consists of those who do not currently have housing and those who are likely to lose their housing some time in the future. Compounding this and affecting future homelessness is the accelerating cost of housing in the United States. In San Diego, California, the home of many oppressed visiting workers (who some say are in this country illegally), the median price of a home approached $700,000 in 2006. It is doubtful that oppressed humyns who do not own a home now will ever own one.

To guarantee housing for sixty million people is not a problem that is easily solved, but the situation is not hopeless. There are actually two problems. The first pertains to the economically marginalized who currently have housing, whether they own, along with mortgage holders, a portion of their homes or rent their housing from oppressive landlords. How do we prevent them from losing their homes? The second problem concerns the severely economically marginalized and differently motivated who do not have housing of any type. How does the government provide homes for this group of oppressed humyns?

The solution to the first problem is relatively easy because no one in this group is actually homeless at this time. Many economically deprived and differently motivated humyns have become homeless because profit-motivated entrepreneurs have converted low-cost housing into condominiums or expensive apartments. In other cases, housing has become unaffordable to the economically marginalized because of cost increases and usurious interest rate increases in adjustable rate mortgages as discussed previously. In all cases, members of the oppressed classes have been evicted from their housing and this is a problem that can be easily solved. The government needs only to make such evictions illegal. The government must develop a plan under which the total of rental payments apply to purchase individual housing units, eventually providing pride of home ownership for the economically deprived. It would then be possible for marginalized classes to realize, along with the economically privileged, the American dream. For those who attained the American Dream but have lost their homes because of the housing crisis of 2008, the government should simply require oppressive mortgage holders to reduce interest to their original rates.

Solving the second problem, providing homes for those who currently have no housing of any type, is more challenging. It was stated previously that between 300,000 and 600,000 oppressed humyns are homeless each night. This range represents a drastic understatement since only those who are in shelters for the homeless or are conveniently available on city streets are counted. There is no doubt that the number is closer to one million humyns. Solving the problem is difficult, but not impossible.

The most immediate need is for temporary housing of any sort, especially when cold weather approaches. The large number of recreational vehicles owned by the privileged classes can fill this need. Owners will be asked to voluntarily contribute their motor homes and travel trailers to needy families. If they do not contribute their vehicles voluntarily, government seizure is recommended. Such seizure is seen as appropriate because the cause is just. Most recreational vehicles have sleeping accommodations for five or more people, but since there are well over one-half million recreational vehicles in use, it would be necessary to house only an average of two people per vehicle. Even so, any type of recreational vehicle provides cramped living quarters at best and should be considered only as temporary shelter. The needy homeless deserve better treatment and should be moved to their own permanent homes as soon as possible.

The minimum acceptable standard for housing the homeless should be home ownership for all oppressed humyns. If the homeless are placed in "projects" or rental units, there is a good chance that they will again be homeless. The tendency is that such housing falls into the hands of profit-hungry oppressors who turn the units into condos or increase rents to more than the oppressed can pay. Ownership assures the economically marginalized a permanent home and provides a high degree of community pride. Humyns who own their homes are better citizens.

The first task is to identify all members of the advantaged classes who own two or more homes. Too many oppressors have homes in the city, in the country, a cottage at the beach and a cabin in the mountains. As long as anyone is homeless, no humyn should be allowed to own more than one home. As responsible members of society, those who own more than one home will willingly give their additional homes to the homeless to provide permanent shelter. As the economically advantaged continue to acquire additional homes, these homes, too, will be given to the homeless. If additional homes owned by the privileged classes are not given freely to the oppressed, government as the chief benefactor of the people will use the power of eminent domain to implement seizure of all such homes. Again, this seizure is seen as appropriate because the cause is just.

Other solutions for the problem of the homeless must be sought in the private sector. One of the major causes of homelessness is discrimination in mortgage lending. A study conducted in 1992 by the Boston Federal Reserve Bank found that black and Hispanic applicants are denied mortgage loans more frequently than are white applicants. It was claimed that this was often due to the fact that blacks and Hispanics have less wealth, savings and more blemishes on their credit records. However, even after controlling for these factors, researchers from the Boston Fed found that minority applicants were more than fifty percent likely to be refused a loan than were white applicants. The denial rate for whites with similar economic and income characteristics as applicants of color was only eleven percent while the denial rate for people of color was seventeen percent. The denial rate for wimyn was not mentioned in the study.

The solution to this part of the problem is obvious. Government must mandate a mortgage approval rate for minorities equal to that of whites! Severe penalties for noncompliance must be prescribed.

However, this solution would address only a very small part of the total problem of homelessness. It would help only those who can afford a home of their own and completely ignore the plight of the economically oppressed who would also like to see their American dreams come true. Once it is accepted that the economically oppressed have been denied for years the American dream of home ownership by economic oppressors, the solution is obvious. In order to atone for past injustices, economic oppressors must enable the economically disadvantaged and differently motivated to own homes of their own. Not only is the solution just, it is a solution with which capitalists will agree since it will be implemented through the private sector market system.

The problem is not always that the economically marginalized cannot afford the price of a new home. What they cannot afford is the price of money. Interest payments on the mortgage loan comprise the major portion of the monthly payment homeowners must make. During the early years of paying for their homes, oppressed homeowners will find that less than twenty-five dollars of a seven hundred dollar payment will be accredited to principal of the loan. The remaining $675 or so is going for interest payments to oppressive bank owners. Interest payments alone will amount to several times the value of the home, increasing the total price paid over time for a modestly priced home to $300,000 or more. It is no wonder the economically disadvantaged routinely fail to realize the American dream.

The solution is simple, obvious and fair. Mortgage interest rates charged home buyers should be based upon ability to pay rather than current market rates. The economically advantaged will pay higher-than-market rates while the economically marginalized will pay lower-than-market rates, with those earning median incomes paying market rates. This system is seen as fair and efficient. It is fair in that no one will pay more than h'orsh' can afford. It is efficient in that the decision point for mortgage applicants is the median income level. Half the mortgage applicants have incomes above the median income and half have incomes below the median. The severely oppressed may receive an interest-free loan in order to buy a home, making monthly principal-only payments. The payment of principal will be extended over a period of thirty years, allowing the oppressed to buy a hundred thousand dollar home with no down payment and a monthly payment of $277.

Rich oppressors will pay a higher rate, but no more than twice the market rate. This means that the "superrich" will be paying interest rates double the market rates, effectively making two interest payments for one mortgage. All interest payments above those required by market rates will be placed in a government-managed fund dedicated to helping economically oppressed humyns realize their American dreams of home ownership. This is also economically efficient in that it is interest-payment neutral. If the deprived pay no interest and the advantaged pay twice the market interest rate, the total amount paid in interest remains the same.

The loophole in the ability-to-pay mortgage rate is obvious. Many rich oppressors have no need for a mortgage. They simply pay cash and therefore avoid the high mortgage interest rates resulting from their incomes. In order to close this loophole, the economically advantaged who pay cash for their homes will be charged a one-time tax equal to the value of the home. For the sake of fairness in taxation, the tax will not exceed the price of a median-priced home. The tax will also be fair because, compared to an interest payment compounded over thirty years, the cost-over-time of the payment will be reduced considerably.

There still remains a problem for the homeless. Some are so disadvantaged that they simply cannot afford to make a principle payment of $200. Yet, they have a right to home ownership. There is no other solution than to establish a government fund to aid these unfortunate humyns. Sympathetic and benevolent taxpayers will be assessed and willingly contribute whatever amount is needed to establish the fund. Each needy person will be given enough money by the government to purchase a new home of median price. The tax payment described in the above paragraph will be used to supplement the fund to buy homes for destitute and unemployed humyns.

An alternative exists which will provide immediate relief for the homeless situation. The bastion of benevolent liberalism, the American University System, has readily available funds in their endowments that, if released to society, would solve the nation's housing problems as soon as housing units can be built. Harvard University had in its endowment 34 billion dollars. Following was Yale University with over $22 billion, Stanford University with over $17 billion, the University of Texas and Princeton University with over $15 billion each. These top five universities have assets of over $103 billion in their endowment funds. At $150,000 per home, this would provide funds necessary to build more than 650,000 homes, more than enough to provide housing for the estimated 300,000 to 600,000 currently in shelters, on the streets, or in homeless camps. It is interesting that three of the universities are Ivy League universities and a third, Stanford, is in California. All of these are extremely liberal in social and political thought and would gladly contribute their excess riches to alleviate the nation's homeless problem. The University of Texas might be hesitant to contribute their endowment to what Texans, as residents of a conservative "red" state, would view as a socialist cause. This would be a case for forceful action by a benevolent government. After all, one of the greatest of benefactors, Senator Hillary Clinton, said, "We are going to take things away from you on behalf of the common good." There is no doubt that the greatest champion of the oppressed, President Barack Obama, will continue the legacy.

CH.14: HEALTH CARE

It has been recently estimated that by the year 2015, twenty percent of total spending in the United States will be for health care. This will amount to over four trillion dollars per year. Obtaining adequate health care will be difficult for even privileged humyns and impossible for the economically marginalized and motivationally challenged. The government must take positive action to solve the twofold problems of American health care: affordability and availability.

The right to adequate health care is a basic constitutional right for every American. The Fourteenth Amendment clearly states that no law shall "abridge the privileges" of any citizen and that no person shall be deprived of "life, liberty and property." The words "privileges" and "life" obviously include adequate medical care. Medical care is a privilege and is necessary to ensure life.

Over forty-five million Americans have no health insurance, and this number grows annually. This should be no surprise, because forty-five million Americans are among the economically disadvantaged and cannot afford to purchase health insurance on their own. Some who are too poor to purchase their own health insurance are lucky enough to have jobs in which health insurance is provided by employers. However, even when the economically oppressed are employed, they most often have jobs that pay only minimum wages with no additional benefits. Some companies that offer health benefits are drastically reducing these benefits and requiring that employees take on a bigger burden in providing either a larger portion or all of their own health insurance. Other companies are eliminating them completely.

The availability of health insurance in the United States is income sensitive: as incomes rise, so does the probability of having health insurance. In general, people have health insurance because they can afford it or because their employers provide it. On the converse, being economically marginalized or unemployed in America means having no health insurance. Having no health insurance means not having adequate health care.

Medicaid is the government program designed to provide health insurance for the economically oppressed. But Medicaid is an unfair program because the government forces oppressed citizens to find jobs under the threat of cutting off all welfare payments after two years. Jobs available to these citizens are low or minimum-wage jobs that offer no benefits. The working poor now earn "too much" to qualify for Medicaid benefits, but not enough to afford a private health insurance plan. The poor oppressed humyn is now without any health care benefits at all.

In addition to being income-sensitive, the availability of health care is also racist. While sixteen percent of all races in American have no health insurance, over twenty percent of people of color are without any health insurance coverage whatever. Those who have less education are less likely to have health insurance, as are those who lack work experience. These groups are less likely to have jobs in which health insurance is a benefit and are heavily populated by oppressed Black and Hispanic humyns.

Age is also a factor. Young adults between the ages of eighteen and twenty-four are less likely than any other group to have health insurance. Humyns in this group think they will not get sick and have feelings of immortality. They see no need for health insurance. It is also true that they cannot afford to pay for health insurance on their own. On the other end, the elderly are more likely to have health insurance than any other group. This has been the result of Medicare, the health insurance program that benefits the elderly at the expense of the young. The high personal taxes necessary to support Medicare is one of the major reasons the young cannot afford their own health care.

In final analysis, however, the major reason that health care is unavailable to many is its cost. During the 1980s and 1990s, total expenditures for health care increased by seventy billion to eighty billion dollars a year, an annual rate of nearly ten percent. During the same period, inflation averaged only three and one-half percent. Spending for health care was six percent of gross domestic product in 1965. By 1990, health care spending had grown to twelve percent of GDP. By the year 2000, spending for health care had increased to only fourteen percent of gross domestic product, but this slight increase is because of economic growth under the Great Benefactor,

President Bill Clinton. Costs of medical care are now increasing at a rate of about nine percent per year. According to the rule of 70s, health care costs will double in less than eight years.

But how much does health care really cost? If we translate the above GDP-related data into dollars, we find that the annual cost of health care in the United Sates increased from less than seven hundred billion dollars in 1990 to about $1.3 trillion by 2000 and over $1.5 trillion in 2002. Individually, Americans spend about five thousand dollars a year for health care. It is no wonder that the oppressed who have no health insurance cannot afford to visit a doctor.

The reasons for obscene increases in health care costs are too numerous to discuss in any depth, nor is such a discussion necessary for our purposes. A brief discussion is appropriate, however, because many of the increases in cost obviously result from exploitation of the economically oppressed by the economically advantaged.

The major cause of the rapid rise in costs of health care is the increase in demand for such care over the past few years. Ironically, the primary reason for the increase in demand is also one of the problems--availability. While fifteen percent of the population does not have health insurance, eighty-five percent do! Remembering the direct relationship between age and income and those having health insurance, the eighty-five percent who have health insurance is composed of the old and rich who have little to do. When idle senior citizens have a cold, they will gladly go to the doctor's office because they know that's where all their friends will be! They will have a nice afternoon visit. After all, when humyns who have health insurance go the doctor, someone else pays the bill. If they had to pay from their own pockets, seniors would stay at home and treat their colds the traditional way, with hot baths and alcoholic spirits.

A closely related reason for increased demand for health care is the aging population. Humyns are living longer. In the very near future, nearly one-fifth of our population will be sixty-five or over. As humyns get older, they require more medical care. Because the elderly comprise a major voting block, our government has eagerly accommodated them with the Medicare program and ensured that they will continue to have cheap health care. Now even the elderly who are not rich can afford, at government expense, to have periodic visits with their friends at the doctor's office. This in itself is not seen as a problem. However, the economically oppressed are equally entitled to visit their friends at the doctor's office.

Medical practitioners are aware of this increased demand for their services and have increased their prices accordingly.

Other problems arise from the supply side. This is obvious, once we accept that physicians, along with being healers and benefactors of humynity, are also business humyns and economic oppressors. Doctors are nearly always the offspring of advantaged families, have never been economically oppressed and have little empathy with those who are. Being accustomed to the better things in life, they intend to remain among the economically and socially advantaged as long as they live. The role of self-interest being a primary characteristic of a market economy, physicians in the United States are often more interested in their own welfare than in the welfare of their patients.

Unlike those in other professions, physicians are in control of the amount of product they deliver. A patient will first be seen by a primary care physician, who will send the patient to a laboratory for a series of tests. At one time the physician owned the laboratory, but that is no longer legal. An associate who would provide a kickback also might have owned it. This would also be illegal if the doctor were caught. Laboratories are now chains owned quite legally by large corporations in which oppressive physicians are major stockholders.

Once laboratory results are available to the primary care physician, the patient will be referred to a specialist who will request further lab tests. The specialist will then sometimes determine that the patient needs to see still another type of specialist for additional diagnosis. The new specialist will request still more lab tests.

After all, this isn't costing the patient very much. Only twenty percent of the total, less for those with supplemental insurance coverage.

Physicians also control the number of their profession who can be legally licensed by the various states. They do this through the physician-controlled American Medical Association that in turn controls state medical boards. As if this were not enough, the American Medical Association can control the number of new physicians who can be educated by determining criteria for accreditation of medical schools.

Having the ability to increase demand while limiting supply is, as any first year economics student is taught, the ideal method for driving up both prices and income. The price of even minimally adequate health care is driven beyond the reach of the economically oppressed. Higher prices present no problem to the economically advantaged who either have health insurance or can afford on their own to pay for medical care. All the while, rich, oppressive doctors enrich themselves even more.

When addressing the state of health care in the United States today, economists are generally concerned with the twin problems of affordability and availability. However, the primary concern of reformers has been affordability and the focus has been reduction of costs within the existing health care delivery system. One popular solution is the health maintenance organization. HMOs contract with employers, unions, insurance companies and individual humyns to provide health care at reduced cost. They offer prepaid health care, rather than the customary fee-for-service payments that are currently made. If participating physicians offer too much health care, especially more than has been paid for, the HMO will lose money. It should go without saying that doctors will have invested heavily in their HMO and certainly don't want to suffer heavy financial loses. HMO management officials also monitor doctors closely to discourage unnecessary medical diagnostic tests and treatment.

As a corollary to the HMO, insurance companies have started using health management organizations that perform "watchdog" functions over the health care of their policyholders. The health management company must approve as "appropriate and necessary" the treatment of patients or the insurance company will withhold payment for treatment.

The problem with both of these is that, while some dollars may be saved, nothing is done to enhance health care availability. One still must still have purchased or have employer-supplied health insurance or have the financial ability to pay the HMO in advance for his or her health care. The health management watchdog also leads to the rather bazaar situation in which some person of unknown and perhaps doubtful experience, who could be as much as two thousand miles removed from the case, is second-guessing an on-scene specialist about what treatment is "appropriate and necessary." If treatment is determined to be inappropriate, then payment for the treatment will be withheld. Decisions about appropriateness and necessity of treatment will almost undoubtedly be made based on profit and loss considerations rather than sound medical analysis.

Another obvious option is that the patient, if h'orsh' wants to recover, must personally pay for the treatment. Insurance companies are certainly willing to save money and increase profits by passing the cost of treatment on to the patient or allowing the patient to die.

Health management organizations do not determine the appropriateness and necessity of treatments for free. While saving health insurance companies expenditures for medical fees, they create another level that siphons money from insurance premiums paid by already oppressed workers. Health maintenance and health management organizations are businesses that operate through the capitalist market. Their sole purpose is the accumulation of obscene profits.

According to current traditional economic thought, affordability is the major problem facing health care in the United States. Every person in the United States is entitled to medical care, as guaranteed by the Constitution. Our primary concern must also be availability. Only through a program implemented and managed by a wise and benevolent government can medical care be affordable and available to all. Canada has implemented a program of national health insurance in which the government provides a package of basic health care to each person at no cost. Many in the United States would like to emulate this system, which is financed by taxes rather than insurance premiums. However, implementation of the Canadian system in the United States would be little more than a refinement and extension of the existing Medicare system, which is financed by special taxes. Such a system would also amplify the problems that currently exist in Medicare. People would abuse the system because someone else is paying. Physicians would also abuse the system by over-diagnosing health problems and over-treatment of illnesses. Doctors would further enrich themselves at the expense of taxpayers as a group. The claim has been made that seventy-four percent of

Canadians are concerned about long waits for emergency room services. The politically correct reject this as propaganda initiated by conservative oppressors.

The greatest of social benefactors, Bill and Hillary Clinton, proposed in 1993 a national health care plan, similar to the Canadian plan, which would have provided free health care for all Americans. Unfortunately, the plan was politicized and rejected for a variety of reasons by Republicans in Congress. They said that it was too liberal when in fact they were jealous because the plan was developed without their input. It was developed in secret, they said. They also said that the plan would have created giant new bureaucracies, required extreme new taxes on American workers that would have harmed the economy and caused over a million jobs to be eliminated, and taken away from American citizens their freedom of choice in health care.

President Obama has proposed a health care plan that contains four major reforms. He would require employers to provide health insurance or contribute to the cost of government funded health care; require all children to have health insurance; allow humyns to choose between government or private health care plans; and expand Medicaid and State Children's Health Insurance Program (SCHIP). Obama's plan is unacceptable to the politically correct in that it allows American health care to remain under control of the oppressive market system.

As a first step toward free health care for all, delivery must be removed from the capitalist market. The market rations goods and services to those who are willing and able to pay. The economically disadvantaged who cannot afford the high cost of seeing a doctor or who do not have employer-provided health insurance are therefore denied their Constitutionally-guaranteed health care. The market is also profit-oriented, which leads to exploitation of the economically disadvantaged by oppressive and wealthy doctors seeking to increase their wealth even further.

The government is seen by the politically correct as the ideal overseer of the provision of health care. Yet, the government should not own all hospitals and clinics. Health care professionals should not work directly for the government because that would be socialism. In accordance with politically correct philosophy, socialism is an undesirable social structure. The health care delivery agency would instead be an independent, self-sufficient, government-owned corporation such as the United States Postal Service. All physicians and other health professionals would be employees of the United States Health Care Delivery Service. Each person in the United States would be provided a basic package of health care benefits, as is currently done in Canada. The benefits would be provided in the form of an insurance program, with premiums paid by employers or (for those either unable or unwilling to work) by the government. Health care would remain in the market, but capitalist forces would not drive this market. The profit motive would not be present to drive up costs. The United States Health Delivery Service (USHDS) would control costs by controlling the salaries of family physicians, specialists and other professionals. All citizens would have equal access to health care, regardless of economic status.

Only when the United States health care delivery system is administered with the reliability and efficiency of the United States Postal Service will health care be affordable and available to all.

CH.15: PRIVATE PROPERTY AND PUBLIC GOODS

Private property is one of the most sacred socioeconomic principles held by capitalist oppressors. That anyone should be prevented from acquiring, holding, using as they see fit, and disposing of valuable items is an inconceivable notion. In fact, private property is the concept through which capitalist oppressors exercise power over the oppressed, for it is only wealthy oppressors who are financially able to own private property. The politically correct position is that *private property*, property owned by individuals who can use or dispense with it as they see fit, should be converted to *public property*, property owned by the community as a whole or the state, which will assure that the advantages of property ownership are distributed equally among all.

Inherent in the concept of private property is something called the "bundle of rights," taught to oppressive law school students in the United States to explain how property can be "owned" by different humyns at the same time. For example, you may be holding and using "your" car, but the title is being held by a capitalist banker who will send a skilled car thief to repossess it if you are delinquent on your payments. A male sex oppressor and his unpaid sex provider may be joint owners of a home along with the mortgage holder and perhaps the holder of a mechanics lien by the builder or one who has done improvements on the home. There may be an easement on the property for a utility line and local governments will exercise control over the property through zoning, building codes and environmental regulations. Governments also retain the right to seize the property of the working economically disadvantaged, and even oppressive middle class homeowners, through condemnation and eminent domain. So in fact, there is really no such thing as completely "private" property.

The idea of private property came into existence early in history when people began to take for themselves what had previously been anybody's, everybody's or nobody's property. Others robbed property owners of their property. Many of today's owners of so-called private property are beneficiaries of such illicit appropriation.

Capitalist oppressors have some influential historical support from the politically incorrect in their advocacy of private property. Greek philosopher Aristotle, mentioned previously for his political correctness, expressed a negative view of common property in his response to Plato's *Republic*. He said, "That which is common to the greatest number has the least care bestowed upon it." He also observed "everybody is inclined to neglect the duty which he expects another to fulfill." In his discussion of problems which arise in common property, Aristotle said that workers "who labor much and get little will necessarily complain of those who labor little and receive or consume much." The conclusion to be drawn from Aristotle is that property common to the community may suffer from lack of care and cause dissension within the community.

Another great advocate of private property was the often-quoted Adam Smith, who is generally regarded as the first modern economist. In *An Inquiry into the Nature and Causes of the Wealth of Nations*, generally known as simply *The Wealth of Nations*, he explains how a nation will become wealthiest if government will just keep its nose out of business and let the market system work. He held that private property is supreme and that "the butcher, the brewer or the baker" will use their property in their own best interests and will be guided as by an "invisible hand" to do those things which will benefit society as a whole. They will produce the things society wants at prices even oppressed humyns can afford. If not, their products will not sell and they will become less economically advantaged.

According to Smith, government has no business in the market and any participation by government is considered interference rather than assistance. Adam Smith saw government as having four functions, all pertaining to private property. Government should first maintain law and order by providing an army to protect property from foreign invaders and a police force to protect property from local hooligans. A judiciary system should be established to punish those who abuse other's private property. The government should provide and regulate a monetary system to enable trade within the market. Finally, as noted briefly in a previous chapter, government should provide the few public facilities or goods that would not be provided through the market. This would include highways, harbors, airports, lighthouses, parks, libraries and other things that are necessary for commerce and quality of life.

Smith was rather opinionated in exactly what public goods are. In order to be considered a true public good, the facility must pass tests of *nonrivalry* and *nonexclusion*. Nonrivalry means that consumption of the good by one does not reduce the amount of the good available to others. If the public good were a pie, then twelve humyns could consume twelve slices but there would be pie available for all other humyns in perpetuity. Nonexclusion means that no one may be excluded from the service for any reason. Everyone can have a slice of pie. No one can be turned away and no one would have to pay for a piece of pie. Humyns are not required to purchase a ticket for admission to any public good.

Using Adam Smith's definition of public goods, it 's pretty easy to see that a true public good will be quite difficult to find. He would question the validity of libraries, parks and highways as public goods. The local library does not have an unlimited supply of books and the number of humyns who can be in the library at one time is limited by the fire department based on the size of the building. State parks have only so many picnic tables and entry fees are required. Those who cannot or will not pay are turned away. Highways can accommodate only so many cars and many highways charge toll fees. Air is certainly a public good because it satisfies both tests and a lighthouse may come close. One ship using the light does not decrease the amount of light available to other ships and certainly no ship can be excluded from using the light. But one must own a ship in order to take advantage of this public facility. The truth is, there is no such thing as a true public good because the economically marginalized cannot afford the entry fee or advantaged oppressors have crowded them out.

In addition to the tests of nonrivalry and nonexclusion, Adam Smith saw an additional constraint to the amount of public goods to be supplied by government. If the good or service could be supplied through the market and a profit made from its sale, then it should not be provided by government. An example of a library for profit is Blockbuster Video, which was so successful in charging its customers a fee to borrow movie videos that the company sponsored a college football bowl game from 1990 to 1993. But with the reading habits of Americans today, it is unlikely that anyone could now become economically advantaged by renting books to other humans for even a small fee. There is therefore a definite need for government-sponsored libraries. If a highway or bridge could be paid for and turn a profit through the collection of tolls, Adam Smith would have it provided through the market rather than by government. The family of a former Alabama governor built a bridge over the intracoastal waterway in south Alabama, charged two bucks for each car going to the beach, operated it for a few years, and then sold it for a dandy profit to the city of Orange Beach, which in turn sold it for a dandy profit to a company in Australia, which sold it to someone else, who sold it back to the city of

Orange Beach. The city sold the bridge to another company, which raised the toll and is now collecting three dollars from each car full of humyns bound for the beach. The city is receiving a portion of the proceeds.

Adam Smith would be proud.

To own private property means to have wealth. Wealth includes land, a home, cars, motorhomes, boats, airplanes, televisions, and all manner of frivolous luxuries. To obtain wealth one must have saved income, and the economically oppressed do not have the ability to save. The richest twenty percent in America earn fifty percent of income and own ninety-five percent of wealth. The poorest forty percent earn only twelve percent of income and own less than one percent of wealth, and possess almost no private property. There is therefore much greater inequality in wealth and private property than in income. While money is the greatest single cause of inequality, ownership of private property is its greatest symptom. It is no wonder that private property would have, in addition to Aristotle, Adam Smith and other politically incorrect supporters, its share of politically correct detractors.

Thorstein Veblen in *The Theory of the Leisure Class* criticized the materialistic society of today in which the economically advantaged try to keep up with or outdo their equally advantaged neighbors. He coined the term "conspicuous consumption," the idea that wealthy humans would buy frivolous luxuries just to show off. Frivolous luxuries such as large cars, yachts, private aircraft and exotic vacations are unavailable to the economic oppressed and contribute nothing to their economic well being. He rightly saw this as a characteristic of the market system and a waste of valuable economic resources.

Karl Marx, the revolutionary known as the father of communism and mentioned earlier as a politically correct economist, is considered one of the greatest economists of the 19th century. There is no doubt that he knew more about capitalism than anyone else at the time, even more than Adam Smith, the father of modern capitalism. Marx saw capitalism as an economy subject to deep cycles of depression and boom, and the demise of private property as inherent in the market system. With each depression, weaker business would expire and the stronger would survive. The more successful, surviving businesses would take the property of businesses that go broke. Former capitalist oppressors would become members of the oppressed proletariat and be forced to work for subsistence wages. The ex-oppressors would gladly join the coming glorious revolution of the working class. With the establishment of the dictatorship of the proletariat, formerly private property would become property of the commune, available to all with nonrivalry and nonexclusion.

Henry George was a political economist who had no formal training in political economics. He had no formal training in anything because he dropped out of school in the seventh grade in his native Philadelphia. He became a cabin boy and sailed around the world, jumping ship in San Francisco on his second voyage. He then went to work as a typesetter and printer. Even without formal education, he had that one great attribute common to all scholars; he was curious and eager to learn. He spent many hours in the public library becoming acquainted with the classical economists. By the time he was twenty-one years old, he wrote for several newspapers and eventually became the owner of the San Francisco Evening Press. In 1877 he completed his book *Progress and Poverty*, which sold over two million copies. In this and an earlier book, he argued that only replacing the current tax structure with a single tax on property could close the ever-increasing gap between the rich and poor. His point was that landowners should not be allowed to get rich just because they were lucky enough to inherit land in a good place, adjacent to Disney World, in The Hamptons, or downtown San Diego, or perhaps where oil or uranium is discovered, or something else happens through sheer luck. Wealth from land, he said, is undeserved and the money received from this good fortune should be taxed away in its entirety. Land becomes valuable only because of the community surrounding it and all rental income coming from the land should be returned to the community. Revenue from land tax would be sufficient to support all government operations and land tax would be the only tax required. George believed that all other taxes are ill conceived because they constrain certain behaviors and are a disincentive to produce. Strangely, this is an opinion held by oppressive conservative administrations who attempt to foster economic growth by cutting taxes of the oppressive economically advantaged. A high income tax discourages working humyns from earning additional income. High sales taxes discourage consumption. A high enough tax on unsafe sex will prevent the spread of AIDS!

206

George believed that certain economic problems result from making land unavailable to those who needed to use it and that excessive land rents were unjustly robbing workers of their meager incomes. He suggested a single tax on land, eliminating all taxes on wages and interest. The single tax would eventually result in common ownership of land, eliminating land as private property.

George thought the best way to implement his single tax policies was through politics. He ran for mayor of New York City and lost a close race, placing second but ahead of the third place Republican candidate Theodore Roosevelt. He planned to run a second time but was in poor health and died before the election. His followers continued to attempt to implement his plans through politics in Delaware, where the "single taxers" tried to take over the governorship and legislature. They were soundly defeated, getting only three percent of the vote. Failing to implement George's policies through politics at the state level, his followers established experimental communities.

Fairhope was settled in Alabama and The Village of Arden was established in Delaware. Fairhope, the first single tax community, was established in 1894 by the "Fairhope Industrial Association," a group of twenty-eight followers of George who wanted to turn his single tax ideas into a "utopian reality." They purchased property on the eastern shore of Mobile bay and divided it into a number of parcels for long-term lease. The community still exists today under guidance of the Fairhope Single Tax Corporation. Corporate officials proudly proclaim that the experiment is working because "downtown makes up only one or two percent of the land area but it can produce twenty percent of tax revenue and thirty percent of employment." This is not surprising since rental payments make up the entirety of city tax revenue and the city is in the business of leasing business and residential property. With rental payments out of reach of the economically depressed, the Single Tax Corporation has become a group of oppressive landowners. In the summer of 2006, the Fairhope Single Tax Corporation granted the Wal-Mart Corporation a 99-year lease in return for a deed tax of $3.75 million. This was done without regard for numerous "Wal-Mart, No" signs appearing on lawns of residential lessees who wanted to preserve the uniqueness of their community. The beautiful city of Fairhope, Alabama now plays host to a 204,000 square-foot Wal-Mart Supercenter.

Residents must still pay county and state taxes in addition to the "single" tax. A major problem is that over recent years a "utopian reality" facing single taxers is that Utopia is disappearing. Increases in land values and speculation has transformed the little city from utopian experiment to an affluent, some residents say snooty, suburb of Mobile with one of the highest living costs in Lower Alabama.

Arden was so successful that it now consists of three villages: Arden, Ardentown and Ardencroft, all founded under the principle of a single tax on community-owned property. Much like Fairhope, the villages have become a center of arts and crafts but on a much smaller scale. The combined population of all three villages is only one thousand humyns. The population of Fairhope is over fifteen thousand humyns and has grown twenty-five percent in five years.

Another planned community in which there would be no private ownership of property was EPCOT in Florida's Walt Disney World. EPCOT, an acronym for "Experimental Prototype Community of Tomorrow," was not established by followers of Henry George but would have operated under similar principles. It would have been home to twenty thousand residents who would pay rent for their homes to the owner, Disney. It was to be a showcase community with businesses and commercial areas, schools, community buildings and recreational areas. It would be a test bed for community planning. Rent for houses would be moderate and there would be no unemployment. EPCOT would be more utopian than anything Henry George could imagine. But it was never to be. Walt Disney died and the Disney Corporation decided it would be more profitable to turn EPCOT into a theme park than a "single tax" community, supported only by rental payments of residents and businesses. Rather than the original "Experimental Prototype Community of Tomorrow," EPCOT now is an acronym for "Every Parent Comes Out Tired." This from an Unnamed Disney worker, or "cast member," as oppressive Disney executives prefer to call their oppressed workers.

While Henry George gave economists food for thought, they saw some problems with a single tax on land rents. Foremost, many thought that a single tax would not provide needed revenue for schools, road maintenance, police and fire protection and other essential services. Another problem is separation of the value of land from the value of its improvements, and who would make improvements on land they did not own? Henry George did generate a lot of humyn thought and he still has a few followers today.

The politically correct see public ownership of land as a partial solution to the economic problems of inequality and poverty. Land is a major component of wealth and, as noted earlier, inequality in wealth is much greater than inequality in income. Single tax advocates have become nothing more than oppressive landowners who lease land to the economically advantaged at prices unaffordable to the economically oppressed. Land is a free gift of nature, a position maintained by the single-taxers and with which the politically correct are in complete agreement. The use of land should therefore be free to all. Land should be public property, free to all and subject to the principles of nonrivalry and nonexclusion. The question is how can this be done?

The answer lies in taking of private property by governments through the expanded use of eminent domain, as authorized by the Supreme Court of the United States on June 23, 2005. On that day the Supreme Court ruled that local governments can use the power of eminent domain to take private property and turn it over to private developers to increase the tax base. This was supposedly an interpretation of the Fifth Amendment to the United States Constitution, which states specifically, "nor shall private property be taken for PUBLIC use, without just compensation" (emphasis mine). This decision had nothing to do with the Constitution. The disputed property in the decision was taken for PRIVATE use, which is not addressed in the constitution. This decision did nothing more than turn boards of county or city commissioners into abusive bureaucrats and oppressive landowners who have probably been enriched by prospective developers prior to condemning the property. Even the politically correct know that government is not always benevolent and sometimes cannot be trusted.

Governments should use the power of eminent domain to take private property for TRUE public use by all humyns. Land and the air above it, the minerals and oil beneath it belong to everyone. No one humyn should become economically advantaged simply because h'orsh' is fortunate or lucky enough to inherit or otherwise gain possession of property which becomes more valuable over time.

This is only the beginning...
OBAMA'S MOUNTING TAX BURDEN

The following table shows a projected burden on American taxpayers caused by the Pelosi/Obama/Reid spending spree. The deficit for 2009 is estimated to be $2 trillion, which is not unreasonable because it increased by $250 billion in just a few days. We believe President Obama when he says that he will reduce the deficit by 50% during his first term. An annual deficit of $750 billion, which may be a gross under assumption, is assumed for his second term. Amounts are in trillions of dollars.

Year Interest	Deficit	Cumulative	Debt	
	trillions (billions)			
2009	$2 T	$2.00	$12	$360
2010	1.66	3.66	13.66	410
2011	1.33	4.99	14.99	450
2012	1.0	5.99	16.0	480
2013	.75	6.75	16.75	500
2014	.75	7.50	17.50	530
2015	.75	8.25	18.25	550
2016	.75	9.00	19.00	570

The Obama deficits are added to the current national debt of $10 trillion to obtain total debt. If left unchecked, the Pelosi/Obama/Reid spending spree will add nine trillion dollars to the national debt, which will total $19,000,000,000,000 at the end of Obama's presidency. The debt will be $63,333 for each person in the United States, most of whom will be on the Obama dole by then and won't be able to pay their share.

Have a nice day!

Visuals

Source: house.gov

Source : Library of Congress, American History
Collection. If you think that's bad imagine what the
lines would look like with 140% unemployment!

Source:state.gov Heart-felt quotation added.

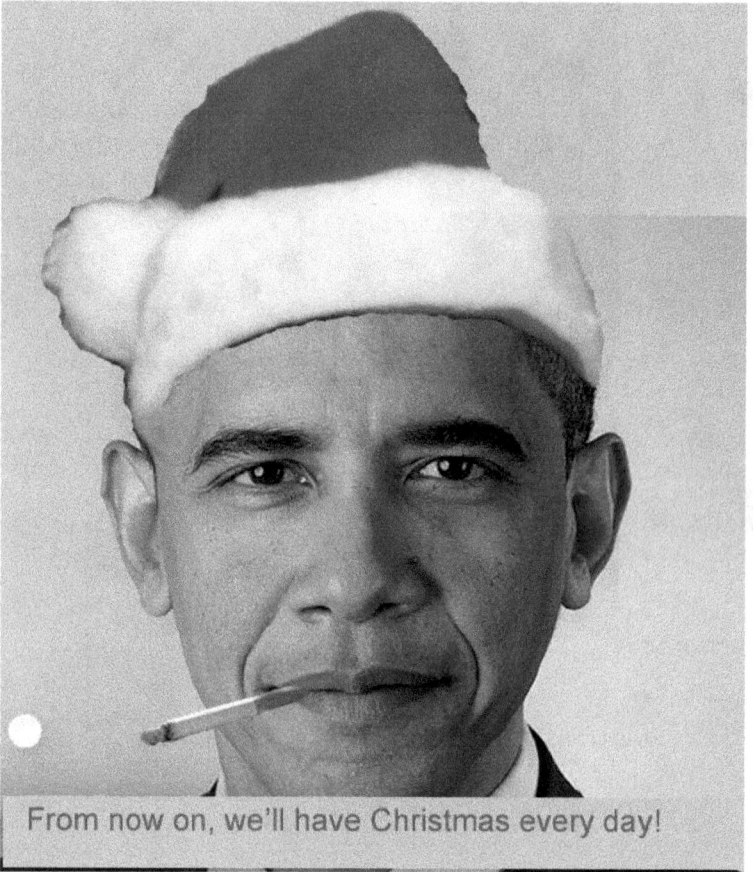

From now on, we'll have Christmas every day!

Source:Whitehouse.gov — embellished to enhance realism.

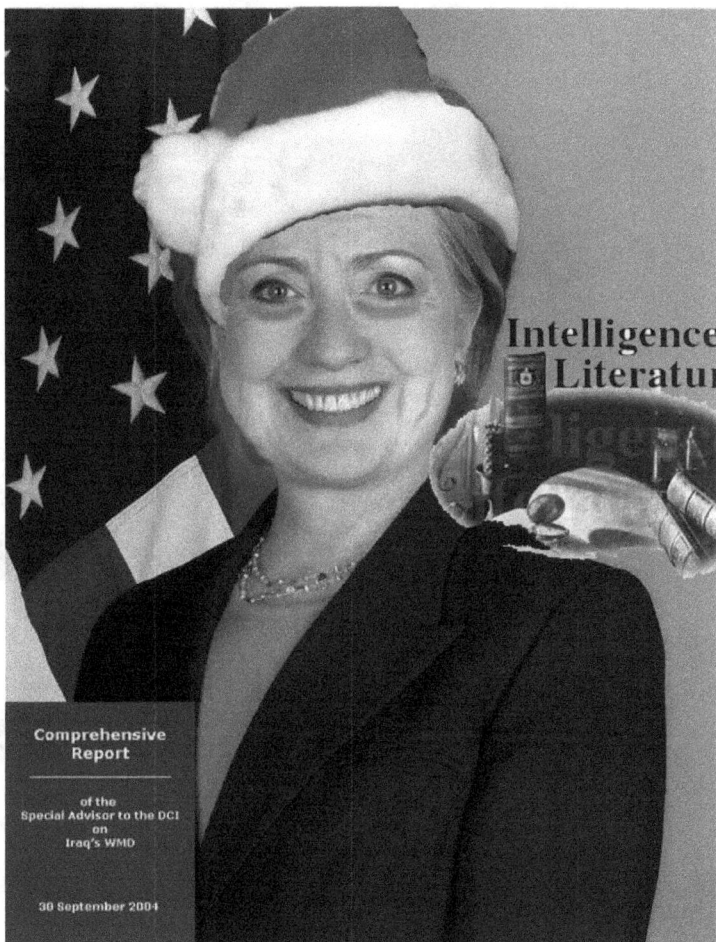

"So, how would you like it if your boss
   called every night at 3 am asking if you
   are "ready" to deal with this crap? Sorry
   I ever approved that ad."

"....Or the one about Christmas presents,
   either."

Source:state.gov, cia.gov

You can fool the press, you can fool the voters, but you can't fool the market-The 2008 Election effect on nvestor confidence.

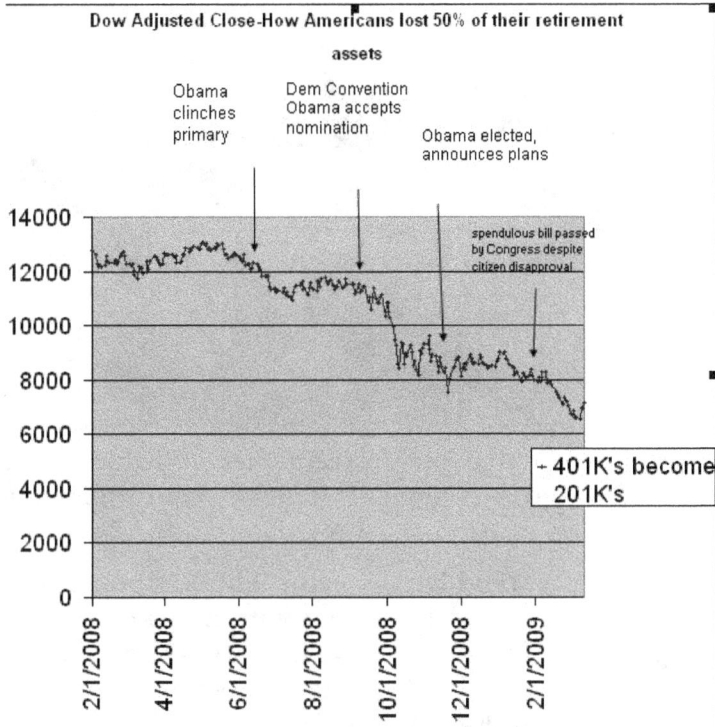

Dow Adjusted Close-How Americans lost 50% of their retirement assets

Obama clinches primary

Dem Convention Obama accepts nomination

Obama elected, announces plans

spendulous bill passed by Congress despite citizen disapproval

-401K's become 201K's

The Dow was over 14,000 in late 2007, before the banks discovered that lending money to people who can't pay it back was a bad idea. Bank bailouts were implemented to ease the "subprime" crisis. Obama commented "It's good to share the wealth," and, "Since when is selfishness a virtue?"

Inflation will eventually obscure this loss and it will be blamed on George Bush. Meanwhile, it reduces unemployment as retirees have to go back to work.

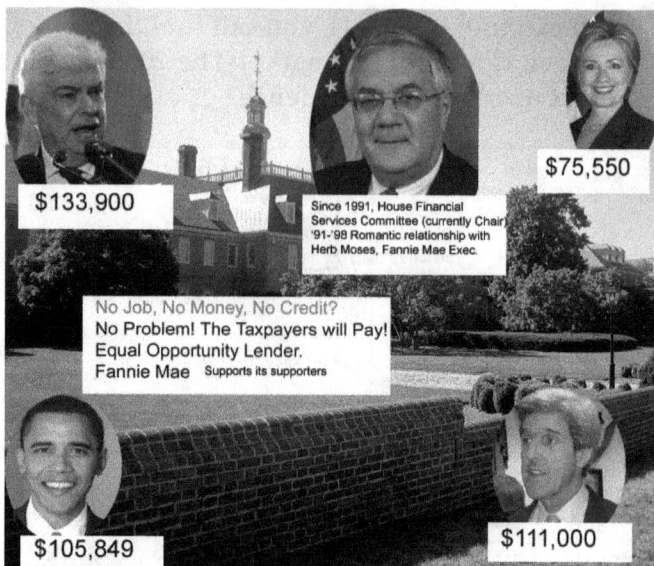

$133,900

$75,550

Since 1991, House Financial Services Committee (currently Chair) '91-'98 Romantic relationship with Herb Moses, Fannie Mae Exec.

No Job, No Money, No Credit? No Problem! The Taxpayers will Pay! Equal Opportunity Lender. Fannie Mae Supports its supporters

$105,849

$111,000

Coincidentally, major recipients of Fannie Mae PAC and employee largess were primary impeders of attempts at regulatory reform.

Obama worked closely with ACORN on various projects such as loosening voting standards and pushing for "less discrimination" on loans. Obama's website, fightthesmears.com was quick to point out that "ACORN never hired Obama as a trainer, organizer, or any type of employee." (he was an unpaid volunteer. In fact, he paid them!)

Dodd and Kerry are legendary long-time skimmers.

Barney Frank very carefully checked out the "background" of at least one Fannie Mae executive as part of the regulation process.

Sources: Wikipedia.org, senate.gov, house.gov

Al Gore, Inventor of the Internet, Internationally renowned expert on hot air and "President-elect" of the United States explains why it would be politically correct to ride bicycles instead of cars from your mansion to the airport where you board your private jet. Gore has set up foreign companies to sell himself "carbon offsets" to reduce his carbon butt print.

Source:nlm.nih.gov

You invented
Surfing?

Al Gore, Inventor of the Internet, Internationally renowned expert on hot air and "President-elect" of the United States explains that politically incorrect energy use has caused the oceans to drown Polar Bears. Fortunately, the population of Polar Bears appears to be holding up quite well. Gore's education consists of a degree in Political Science, an oxymoron. Perhaps he has trouble interpreting data because he had inadequate math and science education.

Source:nara.gov

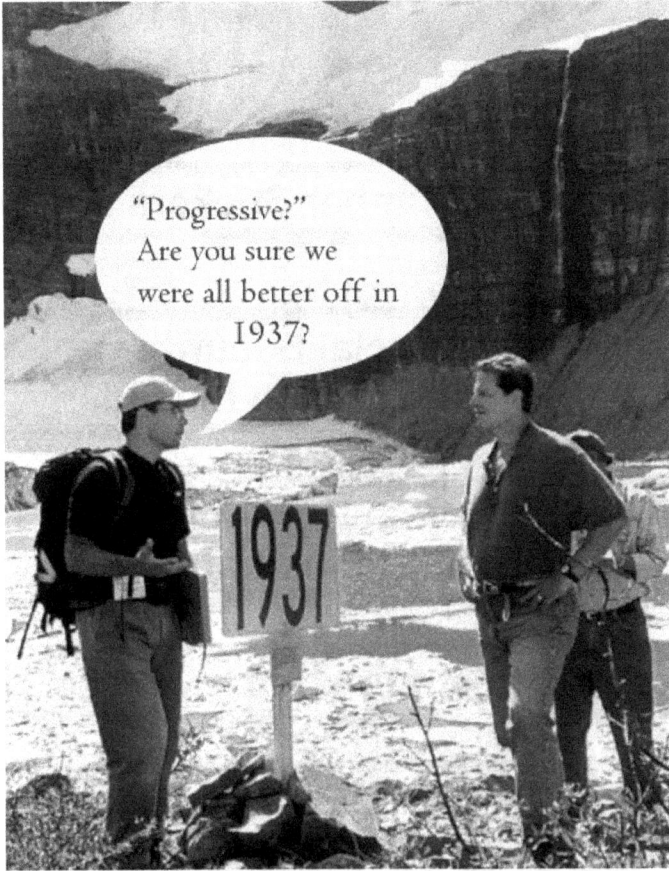

Al Gore explains why it would be politically correct to roll back progress to the conditions of the 1937 Depression so that the world will be colder again. Famines and poverty, as well as killing cold weather would reduce the population. There would be fewer people to exhale carbon dioxide. It's a win-win situation.

Source:nrmsc.usgs.gov

PC Bumper Stickers

Save Social Security--
deny health care to the elderly

Fat Vice Presidents
cause Global Warming

This bus burns baby whales.

"Organic" means
garnished with E. Coli

Don't eat the brown spinach.

The more you stir it
the more it stinks.

Polar Bears eat baby seals.

Polar Bears like it warmer too

Polar Bears breed in summer

Caribou breed better by pipelines.

If you pay people to do stupid stuff, they'll keep doing stupid stuff.

It would be impolite to drug test welfare recipients.

Welfare recipients are twice as likely to smoke cigarettes

Tithe, don't tax-get government out of the "charity" business

It depends on what "illegal" means.

Support equal rights-abolish
EEOC.

I brake for tailgaters.

Brain damage causes
cellphones.

Solve overpopulation -- outlaw
DDT.

Fight over-population --
burn food in your car.

Save the baby mosquitoes.

Preserve mosquito breeding
grounds.

Smallpox is an endangered
species.

Preserve smallpox
for our grandchildren.

Congress has
good spending habits.

Fight diversity -- support
Planned Parenthood.

Vegetarians cause Global
Warming.

Al Gore is the authoritative
source on hot air.

To take the temperature of the
Earth-put the thermometer in Al
Gore.

Save the mosquito -- ban DDT.

Use baby whale biodiesel.

Wind farming controls the bird population.

governments cure medical progress.

Prevent Aging -- socialize medicine

Universal shoe care should be a RIGHT.

Leave petroleum in the ground -- it will eventually get out on its own.

Leave Forests alone --They will eventually burn on their own.

Disseminate mercury -- use Compact fluorescent bulbs.

"Native Americans" came from Asia.

"Plan C" is the plastic bag you get from the dry cleaners

Some change we can "be leavin'."

Collect more overdue taxes by nominating more cabinet members.

It's impolite to pour water up a terrorist's nose. It distracts him from his planning.

ACORN never hired Obama—He was a volunteer trainer.

A Bipartisan Plan to Save America: Get rid of all the liberals in Washington.

Proposed Constitutional Amendment: Congress may appropriate citizens' retirement savings to bailout stupid people.

False Hope gives loose Change.

Cure unemployment—put retirees back to work to pay their new taxes.

Save Social Security: nationalize health care and prevent aging.

The congressional enthusiasm for spending other peoples' money appears to be bipartisan.

"Global Warming" hysteria is a bipartisan boondoggle.

> **Message to Congress: Citizens are to be heard, not herded.**

> **The most important words in the Constitution: "We, the people..."**

See much more in the upcoming book, **Politically Correct Bumper stickers, Wisdom of our Leaders and Other Inspiring Songs and Poems**

About the author, Chuck Holmes

Charles W. Holmes is retired as Professor of Economics at Bainbridge College, a unit of the University System of Georgia. He is also a former Air Force pilot with over 7,000 flying hours and 236 combat missions over Vietnam. He completed his baccalaureate degree while in the Air Force and entered graduate school at Florida State University immediately after retirement. He received his masters degree in 1975, was awarded a teaching fellowship and completed his Ph.D. in 1976.

He then worked as an analyst for the BDM Corp. in Washington, D.C. for four years. Work at BDM involved interaction with bureaucrats of the federal government, primarily those of the Department of Defense. He sought to return to

232

academe and became Director of the Aviation Research Center and Assistant Professor of Economics at Embry-Riddle Aeronautical University of Daytona Beach, Florida. As government and Federal Aviation Administration sponsorship of contractual services declined during the recession of the early 1980s, he accepted an appointment to Bainbridge College, where he taught economics and statistics.

He retired as full professor in the year 2000 after fulfilling his desire to work into the new century.

Chuck is author of several academic and technical works pertaining to education and economics, including economic impact studies and Social Security viability, which are rather esoteric in nature and of little interest to the general public. He was a major investigator and primary author of a study of pilot judgment and has reviewed books for the Southern Political Science Journal.

234

Other Books

Disabilities and Adaptation

HOW TO TRAVEL — A Guidebook for Persons with a Disability – Fred Rosen (1997)

HOW TO TRAVEL in Canada — A Guidebook for A Visitor with a Disability – Fred Rosen (2000) MacroPrintBooks™ edition (2001) ISBN 1-888725-30-3 7X8, 16 pt, 200 pp, $19.95

How to travel to and in Britain & Northern Ireland : a guidebook for visitors with a disability – Fred Rosen (2006) MacroPrintBooks™ edition ISBN 1-888725-48-6, 7X8, 16 pt, 200 pp, $19.95

Sometimes MS is Yucky Kimberly Harrold, Illustrated by Eric Whitfield (2005) Illustrated color booklet for children ages 3-8 who have a parent or loved one with Multiple Sclerosis Includes a "Parent Section" with suggestions on therapeutic activities for providing emotional support to kids dealing with MS in their young lives ISBN 1-59630-006-X Thirty two pp $7.95

AVOIDING Attendants from HELL: A Practical Guide to Finding, Hiring & Keeping Personal Care Attendants 2nd Edn — June Price, (2002), Paperback edition (2002) ISBN 1-888725-60-5, 8¼X6½, 200 pp, $18.95

Biography & History

Virginia Mayo — The Best Years of My Life (2002) Autobiography of film star Virginia Mayo as told to LC Van Savage. From her early days in Vaudeville and the Muny in St Louis to the dozens of hit motion pictures, with dozens of photographs. ISBN 1-888725-53-2, 5½ X 8¼, 200 pp, $16.95

To Norma Jeane With Love, Jimmie -Jim Dougherty as told to LC Van Savage (2001) ISBN 1-888725-51-6 The sensitive and touching story of Jim Dougherty's teenage bride who later became Marilyn Monroe. Dozens of photographs. "The Marilyn Monroe book of the year!" As seen on TV. 5½X8¼, 200 pp, $16.95

Ellos Pasaron por Aqui — 99 New Mexicans and a Few Other Folks (2005) compilation of old-time stories illustrates how the Wild West really was during New Mexico's frontier era. ISBN 1-888725-92-3, 7X10, 260 pp, $16.95

50 Things You Didn't Learn in School–But Should Have: Little known facts that still affect our world today (2005) by John Naese, . ISBN 1-888725-49-4, 5½X8¼, 200 pp, illustrated. $16.95

Bloodville — Don Bullis (2002) Fictional adaptation of the Budville, NM murders by New Mexico crime historian, Don Bullis. 5½ X 8¼, 350 pp ISBN: 1-888725-75-3 $14.95

Journey to a Closed City with the International Executive Service Corps — Russell R. Miller (2004) ISBN 1-888725-94-X, Describes the adventures of a retired executive volunteering with the senior citizens' equivalent of the Peace Corp as he applies his professional skills in a former Iron Curtain city emerging into the dawn of a new economy.This book is essential reading for anyone approaching retirement who is interested in opportunities to exercise skills to "do good" during expense-paid travel to intriguing locations. Journey to A Closed City should also appeal to armchair travelers eager to explore far-off corners of the world in our rapidly-evolving global community. paperback, 5½X8¼,270pp,$16.95

Serious thought and just for fun

Value Centered Leadership — A Survivor's Strategy for Personal and Professional Growth — Captain George A. Burk (2004) Principles of Leadership & Total Quality Management applied to all aspects of living. ISBN 1-888725-59-1, 5½X8¼, 120 pp, $16.95

The Bridge Never Crossed — A Survivor's Search for Meaning. Captain George A. Burk (1999) The inspiring story of George Burk, lone survivor of a military plane crash, who overcame extensive burn injuries to earn a presidential award and become a highly successful motivational speaker. ISBN 1-888725-16-8, 5½X8¼, 170 pp, illustrated. $16.95

Spiritual Journeys in Prayer and Song with music CD, Reverend Peter Unger, 2006. Short Christian meditations with accompanying songs on CD ISBN 1-59630-009-4 (regular print edition) 5½X8¼, 185 pp, $24.95 ISBN 1-59630-010-8

Me and My Shadows — Shadow Puppet Fun for Kids of All Ages — Elizabeth Adams, Revised Edition by Dr. Bud Banis (2000) A thoroughly illustrated guide to the art of shadow puppet entertainment using tools that are always at hand wherever you go. A perfect gift for children and adults. ISBN 1-888725-44-3, 7X8¼, 67 pp, 12.95

Medical

The Stress Myth -Serge Doublet, PhD (2000) A thorough examination of the concept that 'stress' is the source of unexplained afflictions. Debunking mysticism, psychologist Serge Doublet reviews the history of other concepts such as 'demons', 'humors', 'hysteria' and 'neurasthenia' that had been placed in this role in the past, and provides an alternative approach for more success in coping with life's challenges. ISBN 1-888725-36-2, 5½X8¼, 280 pp, $24.95

Plague Legends: from the Miasmas of Hippocrates to the Microbes of Pasteur-Socrates Litsios D.Sc. (2001) Medical progress from early history through the 19th Century in understanding origins and spread of contagious disease. A thorough but readable and enlightening history of medicine. Illustrated, Bibliography, Index ISBN 1-888725-33-8, 6¼X8¼, 250pp, $24.95

Sexually Transmitted Diseases — Symptoms, Diagnosis, Treatment, Prevention-2nd Edition – CDC Staff, Assembled and Edited by R.J.Banis, PhD, (2006) Illustrated with more than 70 figures and photographs of lesions, ISBN 1-888725-58-3, 8¼X5½, 290 pp, $18.95

Contemporary Fiction (also available in large print)

The Gift of the Magic -and other enchanting character-building stories for smart teenage girls who want to grow up to be strong women. Richard Showstack, (2004) 1-888725-64-8 5½ X8¼, 145 pp, $14.95

A Horse Named Peggy-and other enchanting character-building stories for smart teenage boys who want to grow up to be good men. Richard Showstack, (2004) 1-888725-66-4. 5½ X8¼, 145 pp, $14.95

The Cut—John Evans (2003). Football, Mystery and Mayhem in a highschool setting by John Evans ISBN: 1-888725-82-6 5½ X 8¼, 100 pp $14.95

The Job—Eric Whitfield (2001) A story of self-discovery in the context of the death of a grandfather.. A book to read and share in times of change and Grieving. ISBN 1-888725-68-0, 5½ X 8¼, 100 pp, $14.95

Rhythm of the Sea —Shari Cohen (2001). Delightful collection of heartwarming stories of life relationships set in the context of oceans and lakes. Shari Cohen is a popular author of Womens' magazine articles and contributor to the Chicken Soup for the Soul series. ISBN 1-888725-55-9, 8X6.5 150 pp, $14.95

Riverdale Chronicles—Charles F. Rechlin (2003). Life, living and character studies in the setting of the Riverdale Golf Club by Charles F. Rechlin 5½ X 8¼, 100 pp ISBN: 1-888725-84-2 $14.95

Winners and Losers--Charles F. Rechlin (2005). a collection of humorous short stories portraying misadventures of attorneys, stock brokers, and others in the Urban workplace.

ISBN 1-59630-002-7 BeachHouse Books Edition
$14.95

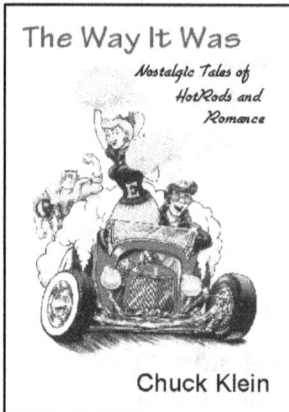

The Way It Was-- Nostalgic Tales of Hotrods and Romance Chuck Klein (2003) Series of hotrod stories by author of Circa 1957 in collaboration with noted illustrator Bill Lutz BeachHouse Books edition 5½ X 8¼, 200 pp ISBN: 1-888725-86-9 $14.95

Lure of the Long-Legged Blond--Norman Mark (2005) A rollicking ride featuring a lovable, intellectually-challenged loser. An hysterical parody of detective tales for mature readers. ISBN 1-888725-57-5, 5½ X 8¼, 188 pp $14.95

Route 66 books by Michael Lund

Growing Up on Route 66 —Michael Lund (2000) ISBN 1-888725-31-1 Novel evoking fond memories of what it was like to grow up alongside "America's Highway" in 20th Century Missouri. (Trade paperback) 5½ X8¼, 260 pp, $14.95

Route 66 Kids —Michael Lund (2002) ISBN 1-888725-70-2 Sequel to *Growing Up on Route 66*, continuing memories of what it was like to grow up alongside "America's Highway" in 20th Century Missouri. (Trade paperback) 5½ X8¼, 270 pp, $14.95

A Left-hander on Route 66--Michael Lund (2003) ISBN 1-888725-88-5. Twenty years after the fact, left-hander Hugh Noone appeals a wrongful conviction that detoured him from "America's Main Street" and put him in jail. But revealing the details of the past and effecting a resolution of his case mean a dramatic rearrangement of his world, including troubled relationships with three women: Linda Roy, Patty Simpson, and Karen Murphy. (Trade paperback) 5½ X8¼, 270 pp, $14.95

Miss Route 66--Michael Lund (2004) ISBN 1-888725-96-6. In the fourth novel of Michael Lund's Route 66 Novel Series, Susan Bell tells the story of her candidacy in Fairfield, Missouri's annual beauty contest. Now married and with teenage children in St. Louis, she recounts her youthful adventure in this small town along "America's Highway." At the same time, she plans a return to Fairfield in order to right injustices she feels were done to some young contestants in the Miss Route 66 Pageant. (Trade paperback) 5½ X8¼, 260 pp, $14.95

Route 66 Spring-- Michael Lund (2004) ISBN: 1-888725-98-2. The lives of four young Missourians are changed when a bottle comes to the surface of one of the state's many natural springs. Inside is a letter written by a girl a dozen years after the end of the Civil War. Lucy Rivers Johns ' epistle contains a sad story of family failure and a powerful plea for help. This message from the last century crystallizes the individual frustrations of Janet Masters, Freddy Sills, Louis Clark, and Roberta Green, another group of Route 66 kids. Their response to the past charts a bold path into the future, a path inspired by the Mother Road itself. (Trade paperback) 5½ X8¼, 270 pp, $14.95.

Route 66 to Vietnam Michael Lund (2004) ISBN 1-59630-000-0 This novel takes characters from earlier works in the Route 66 Novel Series farther west than Los Angeles, official destination of the famous highway, Route 66. Mark Landon and Billy Rhodes find the values they grew up on challenged by America's role in Southeast Asia. But elements of their upbringing represented by the Mother Road also sustain them in ways they could never have anticipated. . (Trade paperback) 5½ X8¼, 270 pp, $14.95. **AudioBook on CD – Route 66 to Vietnam** ISBN: 1-59630-011-6 Michael Lund's fictional commentary from the viewpoint of a draftee. by Michael Lund unabridged 6 CD's --9 hours running time. $24.95

Route 66 Chapel Michael Lund (2004) ISBN 1-59630-012-4. (Trade paperback) 5½ X8¼, 270 pp, $14.95.

Route 66 Choir Route 66 Choir Michael Lund (2010) ISBN 1-59630-058-3. In Route 66 Choir Stanley Measure takes early retirement just before September 11, 2001, and his impulsive decisions participate in an unraveling of confidence in the American way of life. His wife Felicia finds that everything she holds dear is in danger of coming apart: her marriage, her church, her business, and even her country. Who or what can orchestrate the recovery of harmony necessary to sustain the spirit of the Mother Road? (Trade paperback) 5½ X8¼, 270 pp, $14.95.

Check our websites for new books:

Sciencehumanitiespress.com

Beachhousebooks.com

Heuristicbooks.com

Educators Discount Policy

To encourage use of our books for education, educators can purchase three or more books (mixed titles) on our standard discount schedule for resellers. See **sciencehumanitiespress.com/educator/educator.ht ml** for more detail or call

Science & Humanities Press, PO Box 7151, Chesterfield MO 63006-7151   636-394-4950

Our books are guaranteed:

If a book has a defect, or doesn't hold up under normal use, or if you are unhappy in any waywith one of our books, we are interested to know about it and will replace it and credit reasonable return shipping costs. Products with publisher defects (i.e., books with missing pages, etc.) may be returned at any time without authorization. However, we request that you describe the problem, to help us to continuously improve.

Other People's Money

The difference between Charity and Theft. The difference between noble and nefarious

Have you noticed that people who are most generous with your money are most stingy with their own?

Socialists hate private charity, because they want to spend your money on what they want, not on what you want. Voluntary programs are less subject to abuse because the donor can refuse to give. "Entitlements" are a license to demand and to steal.

Socialism produces a nation of leeches "entitled" to use the force of government to help themselves to "free" food, housing, and medical care at your expense. Why work? The solution is to get the government out of the "charity" business.

Don't vote to "give" your money to the politicians, regardless of how noble the cause sounds. Don't approve the use of force to"redistribute income" following the whims of politicians. They have no "Divine Right" to do this to us.

Pay a lot less tax and give more to your favorite church or other voluntary organization. It will be a lot less expensive, and will allow us all to keep control of our resources (otherwise known as "Freedom").

Charity is the American tradition.

Tithe, don't tax.

www.ingramcontent.com/pod-product-compliance
Lightning Source LLC
Chambersburg PA
CBHW072121270326
41931CB00010B/1625